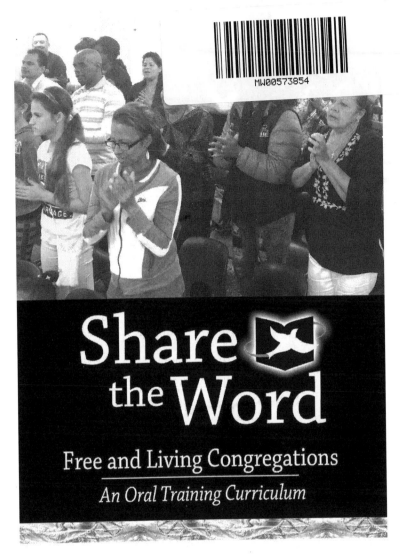

Share the Word

Free and Living Congregations

An Oral Training Curriculum

Dr. Kevin Olson

First Edition, 2017

For information, please e-mail ambassador@aflc.org or contact:

Ambassador Institute ~ USA
3110 E. Medicine Lake Blvd.
Plymouth, MN 55441
763-412-2029
ambassador@aflc.org

ISBN-13: 978-1940508115
ISBN-10: 1940508118
AMBASSADOR INSTITUTE

PREFACE

The style of this Bible study book is different than most Bible study curriculum because the intent of its use is different. This book is intended to be used as a teacher's manual for a person that is leading these lessons in an oral teaching style. Two things that make this training unique is the prominence of the biblical narratives and the questions used to study the text. The biblical text is the center and the core of the curriculum and so it takes first place in every lesson. The questions used to lead the discussion are broken into two parts. The first set of questions, titled *Questions about the Text*, is intended to look deeply at the detail of the text in an exegetical manner. The second set of questions, *Discussion Questions*, is intended to allow the leader to apply the Bible passage to the students. Each lesson also includes an Introduction to the narrative, goals, scripture memory and related scripture references. It is possible to use these lessons in an interactive Bible study format rather than an oral presentation style but it is helpful for the leader to realize the intent for which the book was written.

An oral Bible study format is defined by two main parts. First, the student must learn the text in order to interact with it. Second, the student must study the text with the mindset of applying it to their lives. These two parts are divided up into the following five parts.

1. Tell the Text
2. Retell the Text
3. Walk Through the Text Together
4. Look for the Treasures
5. Take Home the Treasures

Tell The Story – The goal is to memorize the text as a story. A variety of methods can be used to put the text to memory, but this step requires considerable preparation on the part of the teacher so that it is done well. The telling of the story should be a natural portrayal of the narrative including emotion, body language, actions and voice inflections. It should include a short introduction to give the listeners the setting or context. It needs to be an accurate reproduction of the Biblical text because the words that are used will become the Bible that the listener remembers, adding to or taking away from the biblical narrative is adding to or taking away from God's Word.

Retell the Story – The process of oral learning requires repetition. There are a variety of methods that the teacher can use to help the students recall what was said.

- A person could be asked to retell the story
- Two people could tell the story to one another
- A person could read the story
- The story could be put to song

Regardless of the method, the purpose of step two is to build the students' recall of the text.

Walk Through the Story Together – Learning as a group in an oral format requires the group to come together to review and practice their recall of the story. The purpose of this third repetition of the story is to test or show the listeners how much of the narrative they actually remember after going through the story two times. The purpose of the teacher is to prompt the listeners and solicit responses from them. The emotion, body language, and actions all help the listeners recall the words of the text. There are three common ways to encourage the listeners' recall and response.
- Tell small parts of the story and leave blanks for the listeners to fill in.
- Ask questions that cause the listeners to fill in the details of the story.
- Say some statement or fact in the negative and wait for their correction of what should have been said.

These three repetitions of the story share the one purpose of getting the story into the mind of the listener.

Look for the Treasures – The Bible is rich with detail that we easily pass over or do not stop to consider. Looking for the treasures is a process of studying the detail of God's Word and considering what those details mean to the rest of the story. Every story teaches about the Lord and the unity of scripture is seen through common themes. Each biblical narrative comes from a context that includes a setting or background that happens before the story begins and the specific circumstances or situation of the events.

The stories of God's Word include real people who make real mistakes and real people who show incredible faith. The narratives portray emotion, choices, responses and effects that highlight godly and ungodly behavior. Walking through the experiences of the people in the Bible allows the student of God's Word an opportunity to know the Lord and be changed by him.

The greatest treasure of God's Word is the Lord's revelation of Himself. The Bible is one long story of the Lord's pursuit of a relationship with man. From the beginning of God's relationship with

4

Adam and Eve, to the coming of Jesus to earth, God's mission is revealed. By studying God and His interaction with man, the knowledge of God and the doctrines of the Bible are revealed.

Take Home the Treasures – Once the treasures have been found, then they have application to life. The settings and circumstances of biblical times may have been different than life today, but there is a parallel with what people face now. Making the jump from then to now allows the ancient to apply to people's lives.

Even more than the setting and circumstances, the people of the Bible relate to people today. People of every time sin, but some also display great faith. The Bible gives examples of great sinners, some of whom in faith served the Lord.

The ability to live for the Lord can only come from the work of God in a person's life. It comes first through faith in Jesus and the transformation that He works in us. This transformation begins to affect the whole person so that a person's head, heart and hands all begin to be changed. The knowledge of God begins to change the character of the person and that change is lived out in service to others.

May the Lord use these lessons to begin and continue this same transformation within your own heart and soul regardless of the specific method that you use as you study.

Blessings,
Pastor Kevin Olson

TABLE OF CONTENTS

INTRODUCTION

A free and living congregation is made up of people who have been set free from their sin by a living relationship with Jesus Christ. That freedom comes as individuals encounter the Lord through His Word. The Word of God reveals who He is and what He has done. It shows us our sin and brings us forgiveness. That freedom from the past transforms a person into a child of God who responds in worship, prayer, and participation in the Sacraments.

A church is born when believers come together to listen to God's word, worship, pray, and share in the Sacraments. God's Word has practical instructions for the church including understanding what it is that makes up this earthly part of God's kingdom. The church functions like a body with unique parts and gifting. The believers that make up this body have talents that benefit the church as a whole and believers also need the gifts that others have to offer. As the church works together, they are able to proclaim the freedom in Christ and the living relationship with Jesus to others. Through the church, the kingdom of God on earth grows and expands.

A congregation needs organization. Deacons from among the believers are chosen to keep order in the church and to allow those pastors who are called by God the opportunity to focus on the needs of the congregation as a whole. Pastors are entrusted with communicating the Word of God clearly so that the church can grow in the Lord. Pastors also have the responsibility of caring for the spiritual needs of the people which includes administering the sacraments that Jesus instituted.

These lessons include Scripture that focus on the specific topics of the believer, the church, and the leader. This book uses some of the lessons from the previous "Share the Word" curriculum series. These lessons have been chosen for the building up of believers into local congregations. 1 Peter 2:5 describes that we are built up into a spiritual house. "You also, like living stones, are being built into a spiritual house to be a holy priesthood, offering spiritual sacrifices acceptable to God through Jesus Christ." The New Testament congregations and the challenges that they faced are the foundation for the section on the church.

Worship

Lessons 1-13

1.   Power of the Word
Isaiah 55:6-11 & Psalm 19:7-14

Isaiah 55

6 Seek the LORD while he may be found; call on him while he is near.
7 Let the wicked forsake his way and the evil man his thoughts. Let him turn to the LORD, and he will have mercy on him, and to our God, for he will freely pardon.
8 "For my thoughts are not your thoughts, neither are your ways my ways," declares the LORD.
9 "As the heavens are higher than the earth, so are my ways higher than your ways and my thoughts than your thoughts.
10 As the rain and the snow come down from heaven, and do not return to it without watering the earth and making it bud and flourish, so that it yields seed for the sower and bread for the eater,
11 so is my word that goes out from my mouth: It will not return to me empty, but will accomplish what I desire and achieve the purpose for which I sent it.

Psalm 19

7 The law of the LORD is perfect, reviving the soul. The statutes of the LORD are trustworthy, making wise the simple.
8 The precepts of the LORD are right, giving joy to the heart. The commands of the LORD are radiant, giving light to the eyes.
9 The fear of the LORD is pure, enduring forever. The ordinances of the LORD are sure and altogether righteous.
10 They are more precious than gold, than much pure gold; they are sweeter than honey, than honey from the comb.
11 By them is your servant warned; in keeping them there is great reward.
12 Who can discern his errors? Forgive my hidden faults.
13 Keep your servant also from willful sins; may they not rule over me. Then will I be blameless, innocent of great transgression.
14 May the words of my mouth and the meditation of my heart be pleasing in your sight, O LORD, my Rock and my Redeemer.

Study Questions: Power of the Word
Isaiah 55:6-11 & Psalm 19:7-14

Introduction:
The church consists of believers, who are led by the Word of God. We are incapable of coming to faith apart from God's Word. It is the first and primary means that God uses to bring us to salvation. We are never done learning from the Word because it has great power which can penetrate our souls and convict us of sin. Throughout this lesson we will see a common thread that runs throughout the Old Testament and the New Testament as it speaks about the power and effectiveness of the God's Word.

Grace Goals:

Knowledge
- To understand that God is able to speak to the heart of every individual through His Word.
- To understand that the Word of God is able to bring conviction to the hearts of people who hear it.

Attitude
- To believe that God's Word is powerful and can guide His people.
- To trust in the leading of the Spirit of God through that Word.

Actions
- To study Scripture and discern its meaning.
- To obey the Word of God.

Memory Verse:
Hebrews 4:12 "For the word of God is living and active. Sharper than any double-edged sword, it penetrates even to dividing soul and spirit, joints and marrow; it judges the thoughts and attitudes of the heart."

Questions about the Text:
Isaiah 55
1. When are we to seek the Lord? (Isaiah 55:6 While He may be found and while He is near. While we still have breath we live in a day of grace to be able to seek Him.)

2. How can we find the Lord? (Isaiah 55:7, 11 He is found when the wicked forsake their ways and turn to the Lord. He is found in His Word that comes down from heaven.

"For the word of God is living and active. Sharper than any double-edged sword, it penetrates even to dividing soul and spirit, joints and marrow; it judges the thoughts and attitudes of the heart.," Hebrews 4:12)

3. Is it possible to understand God apart from the Word of God? (Isaiah 55:8-9 No, God's thoughts are not our thoughts. His thoughts are higher than our thoughts. It is through His Word that His ways are revealed to us.

    "Is not my word like fire," declares the LORD, "and like a hammer that breaks a rock in pieces?" Jeremiah 23:29.
    "Our gospel came to you not simply with words, but also with power, with the Holy Spirit and with deep conviction," 1 Thessalonians 1:5.
    "My message and my preaching were not with wise and persuasive words, but with a demonstration of the Spirit's power," 1 Corinthians 2:4.)

4. What does God demand of the wicked and unrighteous and what promise does God give them? (Isaiah 55:7, they are to forsake their way and thoughts and turn to the Lord God and He will freely pardon!)

5. How do the rain and snow relate to the Word of God? (Isaiah 55:10-11 The rain and snow water the earth and make it grow. The Word of God brings life to the person who receives it.

    "The grass withers and the flowers fall, but the word of our God endures forever," Isaiah 40:8.)

6. What is the purpose of God's Word? (Isaiah 55:8-11 His Word **reveals** God's thoughts, **brings life** to those who receive it, and **feeds** those who take it in.

    "Your word is a lamp for my feet, a light on my path," Psalm 119:105.
    "I am not ashamed of the Gospel because it is the power of God for salvation," Romans 1:16.
    "Faith comes from hearing the message, and the message is heard through the word about Christ," Romans 10:17.)

Psalm 19

7. What are some of the benefits of the law of the Lord? (Psalm
    19:7-11;

    a. The Law revives the soul – By God's Word we are
        lifted up. "For everything that was written in the past
        was written to teach us, so that through endurance
        and the encouragement of the Scriptures we might
        have hope," Romans 15:4. See also John 8:31-32.

    b. Makes wise the simple – Wisdom is that which
        comes from God. "But these are written that you may
        believe that Jesus is the Christ, the Son of God, and
        that by believing you may have life in his name,"
        John 20:31.

    c. Gives joy to the heart and light to the eyes – "And we
        have the word of the prophets made more certain, and
        you will do well to pay attention to it, as to a light
        shining in a dark place, until the day dawns and the
        morning star rises in your hearts," 2 Peter 1:19.

    d. Endures forever – "I tell you the truth, until heaven
        and earth disappear, not the smallest letter, not the
        least stroke of a pen, will by any means disappear
        from the Law until everything is accomplished,"
        Matthew 5:18.

    e. Your servant warned – We are made aware of our
        sins. "Do not merely listen to the word, and so
        deceive yourselves. Do what it says," James 1:22.)

Application Questions:
Isaiah 55

1. How can we to seek the Lord? (Isaiah 55:6 We primarily seek
    Him through His Word. Worship and prayer are invitations
    from God's Word to communicate with the Lord.)

2. Why do we need to seek the Lord, does He hide from us?
    (Isaiah 55:7, 11 We are the ones that hide from the Lord.
    When we turn from our wickedness He is ready to pardon us
    with His mercy.)

3. How can we understand God's thoughts or His Word? (Isaiah 55:8-9 The Holy Spirit is the one that opens our minds and reveals His Word to us.)

4. How can we turn to the Lord? (Isaiah 55:7 It is just a matter of admitting our sin and asking for His mercy.)

5. Does God shower us with His Word? (Isaiah 55:10-11 The Word of God is readily available to us by many means. The question is whether we receive it. As we allow His Word into our lives it will change us.)

6. What does it mean when God says, "It will not return to Me empty, but will accomplish what I desire"? (Isaiah 55:11 God uses His Word to transform its reader into His likeness. As we read the Word it will do what God intended in our lives.)

7. Have you experienced the power of God's Word?

Psalm 19
8. Which of these benefits have you found in God's Word? (Psalm 19:7-11;
   a. The Law revives the soul –
   b. Makes wise the simple –
   c. Gives joy to the heart and light to the eyes –
   d. Endures forever –
   e. Your servant warned –)

9. What are we called to do with the Word of God? (Psalm 19
   a. Read it – "I have hidden your word in my heart that I might not sin against you," Psalm 119:11.
   b. Delight in it – Psalm 119:16, "I delight in your decrees; I will not neglect your Word."
   c. Obey it – We are called to live in obedience out of thankfulness. "Do not merely listen to the word, and so deceive yourselves. Do what it says," James 1:22.
   d. Meditate on it – prayerfully reading and asking God, the Holy Spirit, to teach us how the Words effect and affect our lives. "Blessed is the man who does not walk in the counsel of the wicked... but his delight is in the law of the LORD, and on his law he meditates day and night." Psalm 1:1-2)

2. Study of the Word
Deuteronomy 6:4-9 & Psalm 119:9-16

Deuteronomy 6

4 Hear, O Israel: The LORD our God, the LORD is one.

5 Love the LORD your God with all your heart and with all your soul and with all your strength.

6 These commandments that I give you today are to be upon your hearts.

7 Impress them on your children. Talk about them when you sit at home and when you walk along the road, when you lie down and when you get up.

8 Tie them as symbols on your hands and bind them on your foreheads.

9 Write them on the doorframes of your houses and on your gates.

Psalm 119

9 How can a young man keep his way pure? By living according to your word.

10 I seek you with all my heart; do not let me stray from your commands.

11 I have hidden your word in my heart that I might not sin against you.

12 Praise be to you, O LORD; teach me your decrees.

13 With my lips I recount all the laws that come from your mouth.

14 I rejoice in following your statutes as one rejoices in great riches.

15 I meditate on your precepts and consider your ways.

16 I delight in your decrees; I will not neglect your word.

Study Questions: Study of the Word
Deuteronomy 6:4-9 & Psalm 119:9-16

Introduction:
Before the people of God were led into the promised land, Moses gave them clear instructions on the importance of learning God's Word. It was to be a part of every day of their lives. The Word of God, which we have been entrusted with for our spiritual growth, is essential for our daily relationship with Jesus. It is in the Word that we know Him in a living way because He is the living Word of God. "The Word became flesh and made His dwelling among us." (John 1:14)

Unfortunately, it is easy to be distracted and occupy our time with many other things besides God's Word. We attempt to rely on our own wisdom and counsel instead of looking in the Bible. The Bible is the very words of God. His Word is unchanging, accurate and applicable through all of time. It is essential to study the Word of God and allow it to be a "lamp unto our feet, and a light unto our path" (Psalm 119:105). The Gospel Word of God is also God's "means of grace. The Gospel is the instrument the Holy Spirit uses to make us spiritually alive, to strengthen our faith, to carry us to Him. (Romans 1:16; Ephesians 6:17; 2 Timothy 3:15-17)

Grace Goals:
> Knowledge
> - To understand that the Word of God's Law is a mirror, curb, and guide for our lives. It shows us our need for God and guides us on the right path. Also, to understand that the Word of God's Gospel is the means the Holy Spirit uses to carry us into a relationship with Jesus.
> - To realize our need to study God's Word daily in order to abide in a close relationship with Him.

> Attitude
> - To hunger for God's Word as daily bread.

> Actions
> - To set aside time daily to read God's Word.
> - To meditate on His Word and His will for our lives.

Memory Verse:
Matthew 4:4 "Jesus answered, "It is written: 'Man does not live on bread alone, but on every word that comes from the mouth of God.'"

15

Questions about the Text:
Deuteronomy 6

1. Why is it important for the people of God to be reminded that the LORD their God is one? (Deut. 6:4, They had left the land of Egypt with their many gods, they had passed through other countries with their many gods, and they were going into a land full of idols.)

2. What makes the LORD God different from all of the other gods? (Deut. 6:4, The word LORD is in capital letters because Yahweh was His covenant name. It was God's covenant given to Abraham, Isaac, and Jacob. It was the name given to Moses on Mount Horeb. That name was the name connected to His Word; which included creation, promises, power, presence, and coming Messiah. He is the eternal, living God.)

3. What does it mean to love the Lord with all our heart, soul, and strength? (Deut. 6:5, It starts with His love for us, the faith he places in our soul, and the strength that He gives us. Because of the life we live, faith that He gives, and His sacrifice we are able to respond.)

4. What are these commandments that he speaks about? (Deut. 6:6, They start with the Ten Commandments that God gave to Moses on Mount Horeb. They include all of the Word of God that had been given to His people; both the instruction and the promises.)

5. How can His Word be upon their hearts? (Deut. 6:6-9, As they meditate on His Word, His Word becomes a dear and treasured part of their being. The Word creates a desire in their heart that flows out into every part of their lives. Joshua 1:8)

6. When is God's Word a part of their lives? (Deut. 6:7-9, His Word is a part of every aspect of their lives. It is the legacy they pass on to their children, their conversation at home and away, from the beginning to the end of the day.)

7. What does it mean to tie God's Word to their hands and their forehead. (Deut. 6:8, It is to guide the thoughts of their minds and everything that they put their hands to do. Strict Jews practice this as a visible reminder. This scripture emphasizes that God's Word is the center of their lives. Acts 17:11)

Psalm 119

8. How can a young man keep his way pure? (Psalm 119:9, This scripture starts out with a very important question and it includes the answer as well. When the Word of God is the foundation for a young person's life, then their life is based on something solid rather than their unstable personal interests.)

9. What does living according to God's Word mean? (Psalm 119:9-10, It means seeking it, following it, and hiding it in our lives. It means that God's Word becomes your great desire and your protection against sin. His living Word, Jesus, is what makes that possible.)

10. Why is there such joy and praise over God's Word? (Psalm 119:12, The Lord reveals Himself to us in His Word. He gives us life, teaches us His ways, and pours out great riches on us through His word.)

11. What does it mean to meditate on God's Word? (Psalm 119:11-16, The words used in this scripture describe what meditate means. These verses describe hiding His word, recounting the laws, rejoicing over them, considering them, delighting and not neglecting them.)

Application Questions:
Deuteronomy 6

1. Why do we need to be reminded that the LORD our God is one? (Deut. 6:4, Our lives are surrounded by many gods, some of which are worshiped openly as gods, others of which are worshiped in our attitudes. The gods of other religions can cause doubts and the gods of possessions, pleasure, and pride can steal our hearts.)

2. How is the LORD God different from the gods of other religions around us? (Deut. 6:4, He created everything and everyone. He desired a relationship with His creation from the very beginning and although man broke that relationship He reconciled man to Himself through Jesus dying on the cross. He is the only God who does things for His creation rather than requiring His creation to serve Him. He is the only living and eternal God.)

3. How do we love the Lord with all our heart, soul, and strength? (Deut. 6:5, We can love the Lord by loving those

17

made in His image with the love that we have received from Him. It starts with forgiving others as we have been forgiven and it includes the unconditional love that the Father has poured out on us.)

4. How can His Word be on our hearts? (Deut. 6:6-9, We must first know His Word before it can be on our hearts. It starts with the Lord putting a desire to know His Word within us and then it grows as His Word becomes a part of every aspect of our lives. "Do not let this Book of the Law depart from your mouth; meditate on it day and night, so that you may be careful to do everything written in it. Then you will be prosperous and successful." Joshua 1:8)

5. What does it look like to teach our children His Word or to talk about it along the road? (Deut. 6:6-9, Passing on the stories from this training is an easy way to begin teaching our children. Asking them questions about the stories will help them personalize it as well. Daily discussions and decisions can all be based on the Word of God. 2 Timothy 3:16-17)

6. Why would we want God's Word to be a part of our lives? (Deut. 6:7-9, God's Word teaches us how to live, how to raise our children, and how to walk along the road of life. His Word teaches us who the Lord is, what he requires, and the way of salvation. His Word carries us on the road to eternal life.)

7. Are we supposed to tie God's Word to our hands and our foreheads? (Deut. 6:8, We do not need an attachment to our hands or foreheads, but we do need to learn, memorize, and meditate on what the Lord teaches us in His word. Without His Word in our lives we are empty of God in our lives. "Now the Bereans were of more noble character than the Thessalonians, for they received the message with great eagerness and examined the Scriptures every day to see if what Paul said was true." Acts 17:11)

Psalm 119
8. How can we keep our way pure? (Psalm 119:9, The Word of God teaches us what purity is, it shows us where we fail, and it leads us to Jesus who is the only one that can make us pure.)

9. How can we live according to God's Word? (Psalm 119:9-10, We can obey what it says. God's people repeatedly disobeyed

His Word which led to punishment and problems, then He sent the living Word to live among them and abide in them. To live according to God's Word begins with His living Word within us.)

10. What does a life of joy and praise over God's Word look like today? (Psalm 119:12, God's Word does give inner joy and peace regardless of outward trials and pain. It gives confident assurance and strength to face the problems of life because God's Word reveals who He is and where He is. His greatness can overflow from us in songs of praise and shouts of joy.)

11. How can we meditate on God's Word? (Psalm 119:11-16, It is possible to read small sections and ponder them all day long. This course emphasizes memorizing scripture and then carefully considering what it says. Recorded scripture is available in audio and video stories. The important thing is taking the time to let God's Word sink deeply into our hearts.)

3. Word as Law
Exodus 20:1-17 & Romans 7:7-12

Exodus 20

[1] And God spoke all these words:

[2] "I am the LORD your God, who brought you out of Egypt, out of the land of slavery.

[3] "You shall have no other gods before me.

[4] "You shall not make for yourself an idol in the form of anything in heaven above or on the earth beneath or in the waters below. [5] You shall not bow down to them or worship them; for I, the LORD your God, am a jealous God, punishing the children for the sin of the fathers to the third and fourth generation of those who hate me, [6] but showing love to a thousand {generations} of those who love me and keep my commandments.

[7] "You shall not misuse the name of the LORD your God, for the LORD will not hold anyone guiltless who misuses his name.

[8] "Remember the Sabbath day by keeping it holy. [9] Six days you shall labor and do all your work, [10] but the seventh day is a Sabbath to the LORD your God. On it you shall not do any work, neither you, nor your son or daughter, nor your manservant or maidservant, nor your animals, nor the alien within your gates. [11] For in six days the LORD made the heavens and the earth, the sea, and all that is in them, but he rested on the seventh day. Therefore the LORD blessed the Sabbath day and made it holy.

[12] "Honor your father and your mother, so that you may live long in the land the LORD your God is giving you.

[13] "You shall not murder.

[14] "You shall not commit adultery.

[15] "You shall not steal.

[16] "You shall not give false testimony against your neighbor.

[17] "You shall not covet your neighbor's house. You shall not covet your neighbor's wife, or his manservant or maidservant, his ox or donkey, or anything that belongs to your neighbor."

7 What shall we say, then? Is the law sin? Certainly not! Indeed I would not have known what sin was except through the law. For I would not have known what coveting really was if the law had not said, "Do not covet."

8 But sin, seizing the opportunity afforded by the commandment, produced in me every kind of covetous desire. For apart from law, sin is dead.

9 Once I was alive apart from law; but when the commandment came, sin sprang to life and I died.

10 I found that the very commandment that was intended to bring life actually brought death.

11 For sin, seizing the opportunity afforded by the commandment, deceived me, and through the commandment put me to death.

12 So then, the law is holy, and the commandment is holy, righteous and good.

Study Questions: Word as Law
Exodus 20:1-17 & Romans 7:7-12

Introduction:
Man is continually seeking how to attain to a certain level of goodness through obedience to the Law. However, the Law of God reveals our fallen nature and shows us the impossibility of achieving righteousness by our own merit. Many try to be righteous by their own deeds, but God has given us His righteous Law to serve as a mirror to show us our sin, a curb to keep us from sin, and a guide to drive us back to our need of Jesus. For whoever keeps the law, yet stumbles at one point is a lawbreaker, and deserving of punishment. God's Law can be found in the Ten Commandments, which are ten summarizing laws that were given to Moses for the instruction of God's people. The Law is a reflection of the character of God and His expectation of perfection. God's Word convicts us with these laws.

Grace Goals:
Knowledge
 - To see where we fall short of God's Holy Law.
 - To understand that God's Word is clear about how God's followers should live.
 - To understand that the Law requires the perfection that only Jesus can meet on our behalf.

Attitude
 - To humble ourselves before the Lord and His law.
 - To believe that we are powerless to perfectly obey the Law in our own strength, but Jesus met it on our behalf.

Actions
 - To obey God's laws, knowing that we are forgiven sinners who are growing toward God's perfection.
 - To live by faith, cleansed from our guilt by Jesus' blood and living in the strength that God gives us.

Memory Verse:
James 2:10-11 "For whoever keeps the whole law and yet stumbles at just one point is guilty of breaking all of it. For He who said, "Do not commit adultery," also said, "Do not murder." If you do not commit adultery but do commit murder, you have become a lawbreaker."

Questions about the Text:

Exodus 20

1. What is the purpose of the Ten Commandments? (Exodus 20:1 It is God's instructions to mankind, the expression of God's holy will. The commandments define sin, they reveal how important it is that Jesus would come to pay for sin and they give direction for how to live. They are also found in Deuteronomy 5:6-21.)

2. What do the first three commandments teach regarding our relationship with God? (Exodus 20:3-11 They define who God is and what it means to worship Him alone.)

3. What do the second set of seven commandments teach regarding our relationship with others? (Exodus 20:12-17 They define how to interact with other people. Breaking the second set of laws breaks our relationship with other people and through that our relationship with God. Breaking any of the commandments means we have broken the first commandment.)

4. What is this law? (This Law is the Word that tells us what God requires us to do, or what we must do to live a holy and perfect life. At creation God gave man a conscience that showed him God's law, but because of sin man's conscience is corrupt. On Mount Sinai He gave His Law on these stones. Galatians 3:10b, Joshua 22:5, Romans 2:15)

5. What is affected when we disobey God's Law? (Exodus 20:3-17. Disobedience to God's Law reflects our broken relationship with God and with one another.)

6. What does it mean to follow these commandments? (It means that God is holy and those He created are to follow these commands completely. We must keep them willingly and perfectly; heart, soul, and mind. In this life, we are unable to keep these Laws, but Christ has kept them in our place.)

7. Who needs to hear the law? Who needs to hear the gospel? (Those that are self-righteous need the Law, those that are broken need the Gospel.)

8. Can we be saved through the law? (No; since the fall in sin, no one can perfectly keep the law. Romans 8:7, 3:20

23

Romans 7

9. What is the purpose of the law? (Romans 7:7 It points out our sins and the wrath of God toward sin, it makes us anxious to seek Jesus and it points out how we should live. Romans 3:20; Galatians 3:24a; Psalm 119:105)

10. Does the Law help us to stop sinning? If not, in what ways does the Law serve to teach us? (7:7; The Law serves to teach us by making declarative statements about how we are to live or not live. The Law of God is the revelation of the holy will of God.)

11. Why is sin dead apart from the law? (7:8; Sin is dead apart from the Law because sin is in and of itself a deviation from the law. Apart from the law, there is nothing to deviate from.)

12. What does it mean to be "alive apart from law" and how did the coming of the commandment cause his death? (6:9; Without the Law there was no conviction of sin. The Law brought Paul the conviction of sin and the realization that he was dead in his sin.)

13. How can the Law be good if it causes us to die? (7:9-10; Our sinful nature is that which separates us from God. When that sin is addressed and killed by the law, one is in the position to hear and receive the Gospel. The Law is good because it expresses God's holy will. See Galatians 2:16.)

14. Why is the Law holy, righteous and good? (7:12; The Law is holy, righteous and good as it is a perfect reflection of God's will and standard.)

15. Why type of death does Paul describe in verse 13? (7:13; The kind of death produced by the Law is a spiritual death which leads to eternal death. Because of the condemning work of the law, we have been separated from God and are unable to do anything in and of ourselves to reconcile that relationship. See James 2:10)

16. What does it mean for sin to "become utterly sinful"? (7:13; That sin is real separation from God, not just a mistake or error, or a little lie.)

Application Questions:

Exodus 20

1. How should the fact that God is the author of His Law affect the way we respond to it? (Exodus 20:1 Knowing that the Law is from God should make us want to obey it. The Law is not just ordinary words spoken by men, but the very words of the Almighty God.)

2. Why did God give us the Ten Commandments? (Exodus 20:1 The Lord gave them to us for our good, not our punishment. These ten commands teach us God's holy will, drive us to Jesus and show us how to live.)

3. Why would we obey God's Law? (Exodus 20:3-17 First because they are God's commands and he tells us to obey. Second, because they are the source of a good and healthy life. We are the first ones to suffer by disobeying them. See also Romans 2:14-15)

4. How do we follow these commandments? (We follow them by fearing and loving God in response to each of the individual commandments. Finally, these commandments are followed and fulfilled only by faith in the righteousness of Christ. See also Matthew 5:17-20)

5. Have you kept the Ten Commandments? If not, what must you do? (No. Repent and believe the Gospel.)

6. Even when we think we have been keeping the whole Law and living a good life according to God's standard, how does Jesus' statement that "there is still one thing we lack" show itself to be true? (Luke 18:22 We are sinful by nature and regardless of the sins we commit or the good we fail to do, we are still first of all sinful in our hearts. See Romans 7:7-8)

Romans 7

7. In defining the law, Martin Luther said in the Formula of Concord, "Everything that reproves sin is and belongs to the law, the peculiar office of which is to reprove sin and to lead to the knowledge of sin." How does that reflect what Paul is saying in Romans 7 about the law?

8. What is it that serves as "the law"? Is it only the 10 commandments? ("The Ten Commandments are only an

25

epitome of the law. Even the passion and the death of Christ are Law insofar as they exhibit the sin and the sins that inflicted suffering and death on Christ." (R.C.H. Lenski, Commentary on Romans, p. 463))

9. Why is it impossible for the Law to bring about salvation? (Romans 7:9 The Law points out our failure before God. It reveals how impossible it is for us to please a holy God.)

10. Why would mankind desire salvation according to the Law? (The nature of man tries to find a way to please God in our own efforts. We try to reach God by our own efforts.)

11. What are some ways that we tend to make sin not seem as bad as it is? (We minimize sin by comparing ourselves to others, concealing what we have done, blaming others, reducing the severity, and by overlooking what we have done.)

12. When do we tend to want to lessen the effects of sin? (When we are found guilty the natural response is to justify ourselves rather than repent and run to Jesus.)

4. Word as Gospel
John 3:1-21

John 3

¹Now there was a man of the Pharisees named Nicodemus, a member of the Jewish ruling council. ²He came to Jesus at night and said, "Rabbi, we know you are a teacher who has come from God. For no one could perform the miraculous signs you are doing if God were not with him." ³In reply Jesus declared, "I tell you the truth, no one can see the kingdom of God unless he is born again." ⁴"How can a man be born when he is old?" Nicodemus asked. "Surely he cannot enter a second time into his mother's womb to be born!"

⁵Jesus answered, "I tell you the truth, no one can enter the kingdom of God unless he is born of water and the Spirit. ⁶Flesh gives birth to flesh, but the Spirit gives birth to spirit. ⁷You should not be surprised at my saying, 'You must be born again.' ⁸The wind blows wherever it pleases. You hear its sound, but you cannot tell where it comes from or where it is going. So it is with everyone born of the Spirit."

⁹"How can this be?" Nicodemus asked. ¹⁰"You are Israel's teacher," said Jesus, "and do you not understand these things? ¹¹I tell you the truth, we speak of what we know, and we testify to what we have seen, but still you people do not accept our testimony. ¹²I have spoken to you of earthly things and you do not believe; how then will you believe if I speak of heavenly things? ¹³No one has ever gone into heaven except the one who came from heaven—the Son of Man. ¹⁴Just as Moses lifted up the snake in the desert, so the Son of Man must be lifted up, ¹⁵that everyone who believes in him may have eternal life.

¹⁶"For God so loved the world that he gave his one and only son, that whoever believes in him shall not perish but have eternal life. ¹⁷For God did not send his son into the world to condemn the world, but to save the world through him. ¹⁸Whoever believes in him is not condemned, but whoever does not believe stands condemned already because he has not believed in the name of God's one and only son. ¹⁹This is the verdict: Light has come into the world, but men loved darkness instead of light because their deeds were evil. ²⁰Everyone who does evil hates the light, and will not come into the light for fear that his deeds will be exposed. ²¹But whoever lives by the truth comes into the light, so that it may be seen plainly that what he has done has been done through God."

Study Questions: Word as Gospel
John 3:1-21

Introduction:
The Pharisees were men who studied God's Law. They knew every detail written in the Law and they spent much time memorizing and examining it. Many were confident that they were faithful followers of the Law of God, and some assumed that they could obey it perfectly. However, they were so focused on obeying the details of the Law that they missed the good news, the Gospel of Jesus. A Pharisee named Nicodemus came to visit Jesus one evening. Jesus explained to him that God loved the world that He gave His one and only Son that whoever believes in Him should not perish but have everlasting life. God's gift was because we could not keep the Law, so Jesus kept it for us. The Gospel is the good news of the grace of God in Jesus Christ our Savior.

Grace Goals:
Knowledge
- To understand that God made a way for us to receive eternal life by believing in His Son.
- To recognize that earning salvation is nothing that we can or could ever do.

Attitude
- To trust in Jesus Christ, as the Son of God, who perfectly fulfilled the law.
- To rejoice in the hope that we have in Jesus.

Actions
- To love the Lord and other people in response to the love that we have been given.
- To live by faith in the Gospel promise of Jesus Christ and not by trying to be saved by obeying the Law.

Memory Verse:
2 Corinthians 5:21 "God made him who had no sin to be sin for us, so that in him we might become the righteousness of God."

Questions about the Text:
1. What is significant about Nicodemus, a member of the Jewish ruling council, coming to Jesus? (John 3:2 Nicodemus came to Jesus at night and he came alone. He was seeking a private and personal meeting with Jesus, which showed his sincere interest in Jesus. It is possible Nicodemus came to Jesus alone

by night because he was afraid of what fellow Pharisees would do and think.)

2. What did Nicodemus recognize about Jesus? (John 3:2 Nicodemus realized that Jesus and His teaching came from God. He acknowledged Jesus' miracles and signs as evidence and he recognized Jesus had answers to questions that he did not understand.)

3. How did Jesus direct Nicodemus to stop looking at outward signs and wonders and to start looking at what is going on spiritually? (John 3:3, Jesus started directing Nicodemus to look at what is going on spiritually by talking about how one may be able to see the Kingdom of God.)

4. Why did Nicodemus' respond with a question about being born again? (John 3:4, He was trying to understand Jesus' answer by man's perspective rather than by God's view. He was trying to figure out scientifically and physically how someone might be able to be born a second time.)

5. How did Jesus redirect Nicodemus' back to the kingdom of God? (John 3:5-6 Instead of talking about being born a second time, He talked about entering the kingdom of God. Jesus knew that the real issue was Nicodemus' desire for eternal life and not the topics of things on this earth.)

6. When Nicodemus asked in verse 9, "How can these things be?", what is He really asking? (Nicodemus was a Pharisee and Pharisees sought to understand what outward sign and work they must do to please God and to earn their salvation. Jesus points Nicodemus to the completed work of God.)

7. Why did Jesus talk about Moses lifting the snake in connection with the Son of Man being lifted up and in connection with the discussion of the way to eternal life? (John 3:14-16 Moses and the Law was the most familiar topic for the Pharisees and they understood that when people looked at the pole they were healed. That would be the same idea with Jesus. It was by faith in Jesus that they would be saved, not by their work. See Numbers 21:4-9)

8. Why did God send His one and only Son? (John 3:16-17 God sent His Son because He loved the world and wanted to save

them, not condemn them.)

9. How are some people condemned, even though God loves them? (John 3:18-19 They have not believed in the name of God's one and only Son.)

10. What do these people choose to love instead of God's one and only Son? (John 3:19 They choose to love darkness.)

11. Why does the man who lives by truth come into the light? (John 3:21 He comes into the light so that people can tell that what he has done has been done through God and not in his own strength.)

Application Questions:
1. How can we see the kingdom of God? (John 3:3-6 We must be born again by water and the Spirit of God. New birth is not is not something that we are able to do on our strength but it is a gift of the Spirit by means of baptism to guide and direct our eyes to the cross. "But God demonstrates His own love for us in this: While we were still sinners, Christ died for us." Romans 5:8)

2. What does a spiritual rebirth look like? (John 3:5-6 A change of life; the birthing of the Spirit of God within us; leaving behind our old self and the taking on the new creation that God makes inside us. "For He has rescued us from the dominion of darkness, and brought us into the kingdom of the Son He loves, in whom we have redemption, the forgiveness of sins," Colossians 1:13-14. See also Isaiah 61:1, Ephesians 2:8-9, and 2 Corinthians 5:17.)

3. How do people respond when they hear the Gospel of rebirth and renewal by the Spirit of God? (John 3:4 Sometimes people respond with skepticism, uncertainty, or disbelief. In our natural self, it is impossible to understand the Gospel. Only by the grace of God and with the help of His Spirit can we begin to understand and accept it. See also 1 Corinthians 15:1-6)

4. When can we respond to Jesus' call to be born again? (John 3:6 Like Nicodemus, we also must be born of the water and the Spirit. That happens we respond to the Word of God, and when we accept the grace of God through baptism and the

Lord's Supper. It is through God's grace that we are able to turn from our sin and to Christ.)

5. How can we respond when we realize that the only way to receive eternal life is by believing in the name of God's Son? (John 3:14-16 We can share this good news with people around us, so that that they can begin to walk in the light instead of in the darkness. See Acts 4:19-20)

6. When we understand that God chose to send His one and only Son for us, what do we learn about our importance to Him? (John 3:16 God showed us that He loves us very much, since He gave all that He could to give us the most important thing that we need.)

7. What is God's desire for mankind? (John 3:17 God desires, not to condemn the world, but rather to save them. "This is good and pleases God our Savior, who wants all men to be saved and to come to a knowledge of the truth. For there is one mediator between God and men, the man Christ Jesus," 1 Timothy 2:3-4. See Colossians 2:13-14, Hebrews 10:10, and 2 Peter 3:9)

8. How can God's great love for mankind affect the way we respond to people who are walking in darkness? (John 3:17-21 We can bring them, no matter what race or religion, to the light of God's truth, because we know that God loves all mankind with an everlasting love, longing for everyone who has the breath of life to know and to walk with Him.)

9. What should our attitude be when we receive praise for what we have done? (John 3:21 We need to realize that it has not been done by our own power, but that it has been done through the power of God through us, so all the glory should go to Him.)

5. God the Father
Psalm 103

Psalm 103

[1] Praise the LORD, O my soul;
all my inmost being, praise his holy name.

[2] Praise the LORD, O my soul,
and forget not all his benefits-

[3] who forgives all your sins
and heals all your diseases,

[4] who redeems your life from the pit
and crowns you with love and compassion,

[5] who satisfies your desires with good things
so that your youth is renewed like the eagle's.

[6] The LORD works righteousness
and justice for all the oppressed.

[7] He made known his ways to Moses,
his deeds to the people of Israel:

[8] The LORD is compassionate and gracious,
slow to anger, abounding in love.

[9] He will not always accuse,
nor will he harbor his anger forever;

[10] He does not treat us as our sins deserve
or repay us according to our iniquities.

[11] For as high as the heavens are above the earth,
so great is his love for those who fear him;

[12] as far as the east is from the west,
so far has he removed our transgressions from us.

[13] As a father has compassion on his children,
so the LORD has compassion on those who fear him;

[14] for he knows how we are formed,
he remembers that we are dust.

[15] As for man, his days are like grass,
he flourishes like a flower of the field;

[16] the wind blows over it and it is gone,
and its place remembers it no more.

[17] But from everlasting to everlasting
the LORD's love is with those who fear him,
and his righteousness with their children's children-

[18] with those who keep his covenant
and remember to obey his precepts.

[19] The LORD has established his throne in heaven,
and his kingdom rules over all.

[20] Praise the LORD, you his angels,
you mighty ones who do his bidding,
who obey his word.

[21] Praise the LORD, all his heavenly hosts,
you his servants who do his will.

[22] Praise the LORD, all his works
everywhere in his dominion.
Praise the LORD, O my soul.

Study Questions: God the Father
Psalm 103

Introduction:
What do you believe about God the Father? "I believe that God has created me and all that exists; that He has given and still preserves to me my body and soul, my eyes and ears, and all my members, my reason and all the powers of my soul, together with food and clothing, home and family, and all my property; that He daily provides abundantly for all the needs of my life, protects me from all danger, and guards and keeps me from all evil; and that He does this purely out of fatherly and divine goodness and mercy, without any merit or worthiness in me; for all of which I am in duty bound to thank, praise, serve, and obey Him. This is most certainly true." (Martin Luther, Small Catechism, The Apostle's Creed)

God has always been faithful to His people throughout all of time. This faithfulness is portrayed in the Bible as existing all the way from the very beginning of creation until the future return of Christ. God is seen as our loving Father, who cares for every one of His children. He is a patient Judge who wants no one to perish, but rather wants all to obey Him and be saved. He is the Mighty God and nothing is impossible for Him! This description gives us a tiny glimpse of the God that we serve. He is the One whose Word we study to learn more about Him.

Grace Goals:
Knowledge
- To begin to understand God the Father's character.
- To recognize God's greatness and His love.
- To realize what the Father has revealed about Himself.

Attitude
- To stand in awe of our Father God and be encouraged by Him.
- To believe that God alone is the ruler of the universe, yet He is also involved in the details of our lives every day.

Actions
- To praise the Lord and fear Him in all things.
- To tell other people about the great God whom we serve.

Memory Verse:
Psalm 18:1-3 "I love you, O LORD, my strength. The LORD is my rock, my fortress and my deliverer; my God is my rock, in whom I take refuge. He is my shield and the horn of my salvation, my stronghold. I

call to the LORD, who is worthy of praise, and I am saved from my enemies."

Questions about the Text:
1. Why does the psalmist command his soul to praise the Lord in the beginning of the psalm? (Psalm 103:1-2 Thinking about the character of God the Father demands a response. As the psalmist lists some of the attributes of the Lord, he must personally respond to the Lord rather than merely acknowledge that God is great.)

2. What are some of the benefits that the Lord gives to His people? (Psalm 103:3-5 He forgives their sins, heals their diseases, redeems their life from the pit, shows them love and compassion, and satisfies their desires with good things in order to restore them, etc.)

3. How did God reveal Himself? (Psalm 103:7 He revealed Himself to Moses and showed His deeds to the people of Israel. God also reveals Himself through His character, His creation and His actions. This revelation that we receive of who God is and what He does is found within the Word of God and anything that we think about God and who He is must be kept in check by what the Scriptures say about Him.)

4. How does the Lord God relate to His people according to the Psalmist? (Psalm 103:8, 13 The Lord is compassionate and gracious, slow to anger, abounding in love. He is like a Father who has compassion on His children. See Luke 11:11-13.)

5. How does the Lord treat us in response to our sins? (Psalm 103:10 He does not treat us as our sins deserve nor repay us according to our iniquities.)

6. How far does God separate our sin from us? (Psalm 103:12 As far as the east is from the west, so far has God separated our sin from us. That is a picture of the freedom Jesus brings through His death on the cross.)

7. How long does the love of God last for His people? (Psalm 103:17 From everlasting to everlasting.)

8. Where is the throne of God and His kingdom established? (Psalm 103:19 In heaven.)

9. Over what does the kingdom of God rule? (Psalm 103:19 The kingdom of God rules over both heaven and earth.)

10. What is the Lord's position in relation to the angels and the heavenly hosts? (Psalm 103:20-21 They are His servants who do His will and He rules over all things.)

Application Questions:

1. Like the psalmist, what should our response be when we realize how great God is? In what ways can we express our response? (Psalm 103:1-2 Our response to God's greatness must be to praise Him and exalt His name. We can show this by expressing praise to Him in prayer, song, and adoration.)

2. Why is it important that the Lord is a God who forgives our sins? What does it show us about God? (Psalm 103:3 It is only through the Lord that there is any hope for forgiveness. The Lord is the only one who has power to fulfill and satisfy His own wrath upon sin. This shows that God has the power to forgive and He longs to forgive and reconcile us to Himself.)

3. What does it mean for God to "satisfy our desires with good things?" (Psalm 103:5 This means that God knows what we need and want. He is able to provide for us. Sometimes God answers our desires for things we think we need with what He knows we need most. See Matthew 6:25-34.)

4. Why is it important to us as believers to know that God chose to reveal Himself and make Himself known? (Psalm 103:7 It shows that God wants to have a relationship with us and that we have a way to know Him, primarily through His Word. He gives us the right to be His children, John 1:12, and to abide with Him, John 15:1-10.)

5. What encouragement is there when we remember that God is a God of compassion? (Psalm 103:8-13 Compassion means that God understands our feelings and our weaknesses. It is important to know that even when we sin, He still loves us and remains faithful to us. We are called to confess our sins, repent

and receive His cleansing.)

6. What does God's role as Father teach us about parenting?
(Psalm 103:13 All of God's character is manifested in His role
as Father. His actions, His attitude and His wisdom are on
behalf of His children. Our children need the same care that
we need from our Father. Hebrews 12:7-11 describes God's
love through discipline)

7. Since God separates our sin from us as far as the east is from
the west, what does He see when He looks at a believer?
(Psalm 103:12 He sees a person who is clean, washed in the
blood of Jesus. As we live and abide in Him and in His
forgiveness, He sees us as being without sin and living
justified before Him.)

8. Can we be sure that God's love will be the same tomorrow as
it is today? (Psalm 103:17 We can always be sure that God
loves us, because the Bible says that His love is from
everlasting to everlasting. Malachi 3:6 says, "I the Lord do not
change." See also 1 John 3:1.)

6. Jesus the Son
Matthew 17:1-13

Matthew 17

[1]After six days Jesus took with him Peter, James and John the brother of James, and led them up a high mountain by themselves. [2]There he was transfigured before them. His face shone like the sun, and his clothes became as white as the light. [3]Just then there appeared before them Moses and Elijah, talking with Jesus.

[4]Peter said to Jesus, "Lord, it is good for us to be here. If you wish, I will put up three shelters—one for you, one for Moses and one for Elijah."

[5]While he was still speaking, a bright cloud enveloped them, and a voice from the cloud said, "This is my Son, whom I love; with him I am well pleased. Listen to him!"

[6]When the disciples heard this, they fell facedown to the ground, terrified. [7]But Jesus came and touched them. "Get up," he said. "Don't be afraid." [8]When they looked up, they saw no one except Jesus.

[9]As they were coming down the mountain, Jesus instructed them, "Don't tell anyone what you have seen, until the Son of Man has been raised from the dead."

[10]The disciples asked him, "Why then do the teachers of the law say that Elijah must come first?"

[11]Jesus replied, "To be sure, Elijah comes and will restore all things. [12]But I tell you, Elijah has already come, and they did not recognize him, but have done to him everything they wished. In the same way the Son of Man is going to suffer at their hands." [13]Then the disciples understood that he was talking to them about John the Baptist.

Study Questions: Jesus the Son
Matthew 17:1-13

Introduction:
What do you believe about Jesus Christ? "I believe that Jesus Christ, true God, begotten of the Father from eternity, and also true Man, born of the Virgin Mary, is my Lord; who has redeemed me, a lost and condemned creature, bought me and freed me from all sins, from death, and from the power of the devil; not with silver and gold, but with His holy and precious blood and with His innocent sufferings and death; in order that I might be His own, live under Him in His kingdom, and serve Him in everlasting righteousness, innocence, and blessedness; even as He is risen from the dead and lives and reigns to all eternity. This is most certainly true." (Martin Luther, Small Catechism, The Apostle's Creed)

At this point in Jesus' ministry, His disciples were beginning to understand who He really is. It was not long before this that Peter had confessed that Jesus is the Christ, the Son of the living God. Jesus had been revealing deeper things to His disciples, including the fact that He would die in Jerusalem at the hands of the chief priests. As part of this growing revelation of Himself, Jesus took His closest disciples, Peter, James, and John, along with him to the top of a high mountain where they would learn more about who He is.

Grace Goals:

Knowledge
- To see that Jesus Christ is the Son of God and the Son of Man.
- To understand the relationship of Jesus to God the Father.
- To know the fulfillment of Jesus as the promised Messiah.
- To realize that Jesus wants to reveal Himself to us.

Attitude
- To trust in Jesus as personal Lord and Savior.
- To be convinced that Jesus Christ is the prophesied and long-awaited Messiah.

Actions
- To live confidently because Jesus' power is in us.
- To tell others that Jesus Christ is King and Lord.

Memory Verse:
Colossians 2:9-10 "For in Christ all the fullness of the Deity lives in bodily form, and you have been given fullness in Christ"

Questions about the Text:

1. Who is Jesus Christ? (The Son of God and the Son of Mary, true God and true man. Matthew 1:20-23, "But after he had considered this, an angel of the Lord appeared to him in a dream and said, 'Joseph son of David, do not be afraid to take Mary home as your wife, because what is conceived in her is from the Holy Spirit. She will give birth to a son, and you are to give him the name Jesus, because He will save His people from their sins.' All this took place to fulfill what the Lord had said through the prophet: 'The virgin will be with child and will give birth to a son, and they will call him Immanuel'- which means, 'God with us.'")

2. Why did Jesus take Peter, James and John with Him to the top of a high mountain? (Matthew 17:1 He revealed Himself to them. God the Father also spoke to them. Parallel accounts are also found in Mark 9:2-13 and Luke 9:28-36)

3. What does Jesus' transfiguration say about Him? (Matthew 17:2 His face shone like the sun; His clothes became as white as light. More than the physical details, it revealed that although Jesus was a man with a physical body, He was also God glorified.)

4. What is significant about Moses and Elijah coming to talk with Jesus? (Matthew 17:3 Jesus' life was directly connected to the Old Testament. It was those Scriptures that prophesied about Jesus. The disciples wanted to honor all of them, but God said, "This is my son, listen to Him." It also shows and proves that there is a resurrection of the dead and that God is in fact a God of the living and not of the dead.)

5. What did Peter think about witnessing this event? (Matthew 17:4 He said, "It is good for us to be here." He thought it would be good to build three shelters.)

6. How did God the Father refer to Jesus and set Him apart from the others? (Matthew 17:5 As God's loved Son, in whom was found great pleasure. God told the disciples to listen to Him.)

7. What does the disciples' response to the voice mean? (Matthew 17:6 God is holy. When He speaks there is no other response. Even the sound of His voice reminded the disciples that they were only men and that He alone is holy and worthy

of respect and obedience.)

8. What is significant about Jesus saying to His disciples "Get up, don't be afraid?" (Matthew 17:7 Although God is holy and fearful, His disciples did not need to be afraid. Jesus Himself was the reason that they did not need to be afraid.)

9. Why would Jesus tell the disciples not to tell anyone what they had seen until Jesus rose from the dead? (Matthew 17:9 It was not time for Jesus to be fully revealed as the Messiah. After the resurrection everything was finished and then it was time to reveal all things.)

10. What does the disciple's question about Elijah say about their understanding? (Matthew 17:3, 10 It shows how little they understood about who Jesus was and what He was sent to do.)

11. What did the disciples finally understand about the Elijah who had been promised? (Matthew 17:13 The disciples realized that the Elijah who was predicted was John the Baptist. They began to hear that Jesus would also have to suffer as John did.)

Application Questions:

1. What are some advantages of having a close group of friends, like Peter, James and John? (Matthew 17:1 Small groups are needed to share intimate experiences. Time in prayer, revealing one's self, listening to God's Word and growing in faith are all part of discipleship. It also gives us opportunity to strengthen each other. See Proverbs 27:17.)

2. How does the description of Jesus from this story affect our understanding of who He is? (Matthew 17:2 He is God's Son, having the fullness of God in bodily form. He deserves all praise, worship, and adoration. "For in Christ all the fullness of the Deity lives in bodily form, and you have been given fullness in Christ, who is the head over every power and authority," Colossians 2:9-10. See John 5:16-18; 10:27-30.)

3. How is Christ both man and God? (Scripture is clear that Jesus is in fact conceived of the virgin Mary (Luke 1:34-35, Galatians 4:4) and yet we also see that Christ is in fact begotten of the Father from eternity (John 1:1; Colossians 2:9.)

4. How can we respond to the majesty of Christ? (Matthew 17:4 We can cherish His greatness, love being in His presence and listen to Him. This means being willing to do whatever He commands.)

5. What can we tell other people about Jesus from this story? (Matthew 17:5 We can say, He is the beloved Son of God and the One that was promised through the prophets. Although He is the Son of God, awesome and brilliant; He is also the Son of Man, compassionate and willing to die on our behalf. John 1:1-4, 14; Philippians 2:5-11; 1 Timothy 2:5-6)

6. How is this different from other religions and their views of Jesus? (Muslims see Jesus as only a prophet. The Jehovah's Witnesses see Jesus as a son of God, but not a part of the trinity of God. Hindus will only add him in the midst of their various gods and worship him as a distant god. The Bible says Jesus is fully God and longs to have a relationship with all mankind; bringing life and salvation. Colossians 2:9-10; Hebrews 1:1-3; John 1:1,14; John 20:31)

7. In what ways can we "listen to Jesus?" (Matthew 17:5 We can listen by studying His Word.)

8. How should we respond when we think of God's holiness? (Matthew 17:6-7 Our response should be to have a reverent fear. By faith in Christ, we do not need to be frightened or reluctant, but we are to have reverence.)

9. What do we learn from Jesus' telling His disciples not to be afraid? (Matthew 17:7 We learn that Jesus wants us to live our lives without fear, realizing that He is with us. 1 John 4:16-18, "God is love. Whoever lives in love lives in God, and God in him. In this way, love is made complete among us so that we will have confidence on the day of judgment, because in this world we are like him. There is no fear in love. But perfect love drives out fear, because fear has to do with punishment. The one who fears is not made perfect in love.")

10. What can we learn from Jesus' clear statement that He would suffer, die and be raised from the dead? (Matthew 17:12, 9 He was clear about His purpose and His mission. It was not to stay on the top of a mountain, but rather to go down, be among

the people, minister to them and save them.)

11. Does Jesus' identity as the long awaited and foretold Messiah clarify our perception of God's plan and how He orchestrates things? (God plans things to the finest and most precise detail as He brings things to fruition, as He also does with our own lives. He is also the coming King, Revelation 19:11-16.)

7.   Holy Spirit
Acts 2:1-8, 11-21

Acts 2

¹When the day of Pentecost came, they were all together in one place.
²Suddenly a sound like the blowing of a violent wind came from
heaven and filled the whole house where they were sitting. ³They saw
what seemed to be tongues of fire that separated and came to rest on
each of them. ⁴All of them were filled with the Holy Spirit and began to
speak in other tongues as the Spirit enabled them.

⁵Now there were staying in Jerusalem God-fearing Jews from every
nation under heaven. ⁶When they heard this sound, a crowd came
together in bewilderment, because each one heard them speaking in his
own language. ⁷Utterly amazed, they asked: "Are not all these men who
are speaking Galileans? ⁸Then how is it that each of us hears them in
his own native language? ¹¹ We hear them declaring the wonders of
God in our own tongues!" ¹²Amazed and perplexed, they asked one
another, "What does this mean?"

¹³Some, however, made fun of them and said, "They have had too
much wine."

¹⁴Then Peter stood up with the Eleven, raised his voice and addressed
the crowd: "Fellow Jews and all of you who live in Jerusalem, let me
explain this to you; listen carefully to what I say. ¹⁵These men are not
drunk, as you suppose. It's only nine in the morning! ¹⁶No, this is what
was spoken by the prophet Joel:
¹⁷ "'In the last days, God says, I will pour out my Spirit on all people.
  Your sons and daughters will prophesy, your young men will see
visions, your old men will dream dreams.
¹⁸Even on my servants, both men and women, I will pour out my Spirit
in those days, and they will prophesy.
¹⁹I will show wonders in the heaven above and signs on the earth
below, blood and fire and billows of smoke.
²⁰The sun will be turned to darkness and the moon to blood
    before the coming of the great and glorious day of the Lord.
²¹And everyone who calls on the name of the Lord will be saved.'

Study Questions: Holy Spirit
Acts 2:1-8, 11-21

Introduction:
What do you believe about the Holy Spirit? " I believe that I cannot by my own reason or strength believe in Jesus Christ my Lord or come to Him; but the Holy Spirit has called me through the Gospel, enlightened me with His gifts, and sanctified and preserved me in the true faith; in like manner as He calls, gathers, enlightens, and sanctifies the whole Christian Church on earth, and preserves it in union with Jesus Christ in the one true faith; in this Christian Church, He daily forgives abundantly all my sins and the sins of all believers, and at the last day will raise up me and all the dead and will grant everlasting life to me and to all who believe in Christ. This is most certainly true." (Martin Luther, Small Catechism, The Apostle's Creed)

After Jesus' resurrection, He stayed on earth for forty days before He ascended into heaven. During this time, He appeared many times to His disciples to prove that He was alive and to teach them more about the kingdom of God. Jesus told them to wait in Jerusalem until the Father sent the Holy Spirit, who would go before them and guide them into all truth. Then Jesus returned to heaven. As Acts 2 begins, the disciples were waiting in Jerusalem for the Holy Spirit to come, living in the truth of Jesus' resurrection. The Holy Spirit came on the fiftieth day after Easter, on the First Fruit Harvest Festival of Pentecost. When the Holy Spirit filled them, they found they had a new vigor to spread the word about the Lord to the world.

Grace Goals:

Knowledge
- To understand the power of the Holy Spirit in our lives.
- To know all who call upon the name of the Lord will be saved.

Attitude
- To believe that the Holy Spirit can use simple and ordinary men to accomplish God's purposes.
- To trust in the Holy Spirit for salvation, power, conviction of sin and encouragement.
- To believe that our actions cannot save us, but that calling on the name of the Lord can.

Actions
- To proclaim the Word of the Lord with confidence, knowing that the Holy Spirit will use it to speak to people.

Memory Verse:
John 16:13 "But when he, the Spirit of truth, comes, He will guide you into all truth."

Questions about the Text:
1. What is significant about this day of Pentecost? (Acts 2:1 It was a harvest festival of the First Fruits and the believers were all meeting together in one place in Jerusalem.)

2. How is the coming of the Holy Spirit described? (Acts 2:2-4 The sound of a violent blowing wind from heaven that filled the whole house. It came as tongues of fire, rested on each one of them and filled them. This is the only time that the Bible describes the Holy Spirit coming in this way.)

3. What does being filled with the Holy Spirit mean and what happened as a result of the filling of the Holy Spirit? (Acts 2:4 There appeared tongues of fire which rested on each one of them, and they were filled with the Holy Spirit so that they began to speak in other tongues as the Spirit enabled them. See also Ephesians 5:18; 1 Corinthians 6:19-20; Romans 8:9-11; Acts 4:31; Galatians 5:22-23)

4. What does speaking in tongues mean and what is significant about speaking in other tongues in Jerusalem at this time? (Acts 2:5 This story describes speaking in tongues as speaking in the languages of the other nations (see verses 6,8). At this time, God-fearing Jews from every nation under heaven were there and each one could understand the disciples' message of salvation.)

5. Why were the God-fearing Jews that were in Jerusalem bewildered by what they heard? (Acts 2:6 They heard the believers speaking to them in their own native languages.)

6. What did the Jews observe about the believers? (Acts 2:7-11 The believers were Galileans, yet they were speaking in multiple languages, proclaiming the wonders of God.)

7. Why did the Jews make fun of the believers? (Acts 2:13 The Jews were amazed, perplexed and did not understand what was going on.)

8. What does Peter's address say? (Acts 2:14-15 These men are not drunk, but God's prophecy about the last days was taking place.)

9. What does Joel's prophecy about the last days say about the Spirit? (Acts 2:16-17 That the Spirit of God will be poured out on all people.)

10. What is the role of the Holy Spirit from this text? (The Holy Spirit filled them. He enabled them to speak in various languages. He gave Peter the words to say and the understanding of the prophecy from Joel. John 16:7-13 describes the role of the Spirit as a counselor, a guide into all truth, and the one who convicts us of sin. See also Hebrews 3:15 and 1 Thessalonians 5:19)

11. What does Joel's prophecy say will result from the Spirit of God being poured out on all people? (Acts 2:21 God will pour out His Spirit, people will prophecy, signs will occur and all that call on the name of the Lord will be saved.)

Application Questions:
1. Who is the Holy Spirit and what is His work? (The Holy Spirit is true God together with the Father and the Son. See 1 Corinthians 2:10, 3:16; John 15:26. In Acts 5:3,4, Peter indicates that when Ananias lied to the Spirit (verse 3), he lied to God, indicating that the Spirit is God. His work is to call, enlighten, sanctify, and preserve.)

2. How does the Holy Spirit call us? (The Holy Spirit calls us by awakening in our hearts a deep sense of sin and by inviting us to receive the grace of God in Christ. See John 16:8-9; 1 Corinthians 2:12,13; 2 Thessalonians 2:13.)

3. Why is Pentecost a significant day for us? (Acts 2:1 It is the beginning of the New Testament Church. It is the day when God's Spirit came to live in us. "But you will receive power when the Holy Spirit comes on you; and you will be my witnesses in Jerusalem, and in all Judea and Samaria, and to the ends of the earth." Acts 1:8)

4. What do we learn from this story about how the Holy Spirit comes to us believers? (Acts 2:2-3 The Holy Spirit comes to

us personally. He fills us, gives us gifts and reveals spiritual things to us. He comes as our helper and counselor. He longs to walk with us and commune with us through life. See also Matthew 10:17-20 and John 14:15-27)

5. What does this manifestation of the Holy Spirit teach us about who He is? (Acts 2:2-4 He is the essence of the Invisible God including the power of God and the wonders of God. In John 16:7 Jesus says that He would send the Spirit who would convict the world of sin.)

6. In what ways is it encouraging that the Holy Spirit comes and dwells in us? (Acts 2:4 It encourages us as we realize that it is no longer only our own sinful nature that is in us but rather the Spirit of God living and reigning through our lives. He is the One that will guide our lives, John 16:13-15. Through Him we are a temple of God, 1 Corinthians 6:19-20.)

7. What is the Holy Spirit able to do through our lives? (Acts 2:4 The Holy Spirit is able to take our lives and use us in any way He chooses, even supernaturally, in order to bring Him glory. He teaches through God's Word, comes to us in baptism, and gives us power to be His witnesses, Acts 1:8)

8. Who is the Holy Spirit able to use? (Acts 2:7 The Holy Spirit is able to use the most simple and uneducated persons in order to proclaim His message with all the truth, excitement, and unction that His Word deserves. This often gives God more glory, because those that He uses are unable to take credit for themselves (1 Corinthians 1:27-29). He is the one that gives us the gifts of the Spirit, (Galatians 5:22-23). Within the congregation we honor and cherish the spiritual gifts which the Lord gives to build it up, and seek to stimulate and encourage their use.)

9. What does this historical event encourage us as believers to do in response of the giving of the Holy Spirit? (Acts 2:11, 17-21 The Holy Spirit enabled the disciples to be God's witnesses (Acts 1:8) and to proclaim the wonders of God. The Spirit was a fulfillment of prophecy and we can invite people to call on the name of the Lord for salvation. The Holy Spirit fills us, Ephesians 5:18; Romans 8:9-11.)

10. How can we be standing up for what we know to be true and remain in our convictions even in the midst of criticism and/or persecution? (Acts 2:14-15 We can stand for what we know to be the truth by being firmly planted in the Word of God, empowered by the Holy Spirit and able to correctly handle the Word of truth.)

11. How can we proclaim the promise that "everyone who calls on the name of the Lord will be saved?" (Acts 2:21 By actively sharing our faith, taking every opportunity to share Jesus Christ by the power of the Holy Spirit, leaving the results up to God.)

8. Worship
John 4:19-26 & Psalm 100

John 4

[19]"Sir," the woman said, "I can see that you are a prophet. [20]Our fathers worshiped on this mountain, but you Jews claim that the place where we must worship is in Jerusalem."

[21]Jesus declared, "Believe me, woman, a time is coming when you will worship the Father neither on this mountain nor in Jerusalem. [22]You Samaritans worship what you do not know; we worship what we do know, for salvation is from the Jews. [23]Yet a time is coming and has now come when the true worshipers will worship the Father in spirit and truth, for they are the kind of worshipers the Father seeks. [24]God is spirit, and his worshipers must worship in spirit and in truth."

[25]The woman said, "I know that Messiah" (called Christ) "is coming. When he comes, he will explain everything to us."

[26]Then Jesus declared, "I who speak to you am he."

Psalm 100

1 Shout for joy to the LORD, all the earth.
2 Worship the LORD with gladness; come before him with joyful songs.
3 Know that the LORD is God. It is he who made us, and we are his; we are his people, the sheep of his pasture.
4 Enter his gates with thanksgiving and his courts with praise; give thanks to him and praise his name.
5 For the LORD is good and his love endures forever; his faithfulness continues through all generations.

Study Questions: Worship
John 4:19-26 & Psalm 100

Introduction:
Worship is often confused with singing songs and praising the Lord, but worship is much more. Worship is a lifestyle. It includes praising God with our voices and all other aspects of our relationship with the Lord as well. Our interaction with others and the way we live our daily lives are also part of worship. Worship is the dedication of everything in our lives to the Lord. It means bringing honor and glory to God in everything we do! (John 17:4)

When Jesus was in Samaria, He began talking with a woman who had come out to the well to get water. He began to talk with her about the gift of God, living water. He spoke to her about her personal life as well as the topic of worship. This Samaritan woman's life changed from worshiping what she did not know to worshiping Jesus, the Messiah.

Grace Goals:
Knowledge
- To understand that worship is a lifestyle. It is a life lived for the Lord's glory.
- To recognize the importance of worshiping in spirit and in truth; connecting both the emotional response and the truth of God's Word.

Attitude
- To have the deep joy that comes from the overflowing living water of a relationship with Jesus.

Actions
- To allow the Holy Spirit to take control of our lives.
- To "offer your bodies as a living sacrifice, holy and pleasing to God—this is your true and proper worship."

Memory Verse:
Colossians 3:15-17 "Let the peace of Christ rule in your hearts, since as members of one body you were called to peace. And be thankful. Let the word of Christ dwell in you richly as you teach and admonish one another with all wisdom, and as you sing psalms, hymns and spiritual songs with gratitude in your hearts to God. And whatever you do, whether in word or deed, do it all in the name of the Lord Jesus, giving thanks to God the Father through him."

Questions about the Text:
John 4

1. How does this woman initially define worship? (John 4:19-20 She recognizes Jesus as a prophet or a man who speaks for God. She considers that worship is defined by a location, a style, and a culture.)

2. What does the woman use as an excuse or barrier that she presents to Jesus? (John 4:19-20 She points to the differences between the Samaritans and the Jews and their perceptions of worship or the religious aspects of worship.)

3. What does Jesus tell the woman regarding worship? (John 4:21-25 Worship is not about a place or a religion. Worship is a response to what the Lord has done to bring salvation and the truth of God's Word. Jesus also said that true worshipers would worship the Father in spirit and in truth in contrast to religious duty or obligation.)

4. Summarize some challenges that this text describes to living intentionally for the Lord? (John 4:6-22 Some of the challenges include: physical exhaustion, social barriers, mental barriers, selfish thoughts, artificial boundaries and a lack of knowledge.)

5. What does Jesus say by stating that the "Samaritans worship what they do not know but the Jews worship what they do know, for salvation is from the Jews?" (Worship without knowledge of the One who is being worshiped is empty. True worship begins with the salvation of the Lord. Scriptures are filled with worship that is a response to God's action.)

6. What is significant in Jesus statement that He is the Messiah? (John 4:25-26 He is the one to be worshiped. He has the authority to "explain everything" to her, He knows what true worship is and she doesn't need to wait any longer.)

7. Why does Jesus declare, "I who speak to you am he." (Clarity on the whole topic of worship finally comes down to Jesus. He is the center and the heart of worship.)

Psalm 100

8. How is the psalmist's worship described here? (Psalm 100:1 Shouts of joy, worship, gladness, singing, thanksgiving, and praise)

9. What is the reason the psalmist gives for such an excited response of worship? (Psalm 100:3, 5 The Lord is God, He created us, we are His people, He is good, His love endures forever, He is faithful through all the generations.)

10. Why does knowing the Lord bring about such an amazing response? (Psalm 100:3 The Lord is the covenant God. He led His people through all of the biblical history. He is the creator God. Our existence depends on Him alone. He is the redeemer God. He has purchased His people from sin. He is the caring God. His goodness, love and faithfulness are unmatched in all of the world.)

11. Of what does worship of Him consist? (Psalm 100:4 It includes thanksgiving for what He has done, praise for who he is, proclamation for all who would listen, and relationship for those who are in His fold. It includes both vertical and horizontal aspects. It is a message for those present and those in the future.)

Application Questions:
John 4

1. What is worship? (To praise, adore, honor, and respect God in our words and actions. Romans 12:1 describes it as being "a living sacrifice which is your spiritual act of worship.")

2. How do the paths we choose affect how our life is lived for the Lord? (John 4:4 We can choose paths that bring us into ministry situations or we can avoid them. We can choose to worship or we can avoid it. We can seek to be obedient to the Lord or we can live in disobedience.)

3. Who is to be involved in worship? Should there be any distinctions or discriminations? (John 4:9 Worship is something that should include men, women, and children from every race or background, because in Christ we are all part of one body.)

4. How does living water relate to worship? (John 4:10 Worship is a response that comes from a personal relationship with Jesus. He gives the water of life; it is renewing and refreshing.)

5. What false barriers or distractions do we have in regard to worship? (John 4:11 We can have many mental barriers to seeking and worshiping God, as well as things that distract us from living for the Lord. Satan, ourselves and other gods are all distractions to true worship. Exodus 20:3-6; Matthew 4:8-10)

6. What types of selfish motivations get in the way of our worship to the Lord? (John 4:15 We can have an attitude that worship is about us and what we feel rather than about God. Hebrews 10:25 says, "Let us not give up meeting together, as some are in the habit of doing, but let us encourage one another—and all the more as you see the Day approaching.")

7. What reasons do we have to worship the Lord God? (John 4:13-19 We have many reasons to worship and praise the Lord God, primarily for our salvation, but also for His character. He is all knowing, all powerful, everywhere present, and merciful and gracious.)

8. Does it matter where we meet for worship? Why? (John 4:21 The place does not matter as God is Spirit and is not confined by temples made by human hands. He is everywhere and so He may be praised and worshiped everywhere. However, He cannot be worshiped apart from the Word and Sacraments, because it is in the Word and Sacraments that God comes to us as the gracious God.)

9. How do we worship without knowledge today? (John 4:22 We can build worship around an emotional response rather than a real knowledge of who the Lord is. We can be repetitious and loud, even with tears, but not acknowledge the salvation of the Lord.)

10. Why must we as the worshipers of God worship in spirit and in truth? (John 4:23-24 Because God is Spirit and Truth.)

11. What reason does Jesus give us in this passage of why we should praise and adore Him? (John 4:26 As Jesus plainly

stated that He was the Messiah who was to come, we can worship and adore Him as the One who has come to save us from our sins.)

Psalm 100

12. How are we encouraged to worship? (Psalm 100:1 With enthusiasm, joy, thanksgiving and praise. It is a picture of uncontainable excitement.)

13. What reasons do we have for worship? (Psalm 100:3, 5 The same Almighty God that the psalmist worship is the one that is still active today! He is still in control even if we feel out of control. He made everything good that we can see, feel, and touch. He still gives us the right to be His children. He is still good, loving, and faithful to our generation as well.)

14. How does our response compare to the psalmist's? (Psalm 100:3 It is easy to take the greatness of God for granted. We can become apathetic about what He has done for us. It is even possible for us to get angry at God because things don't go the way we want. It is impossible for us to completely grasp the greatness of God, but the psalmist reminds us to worship with our whole heart.)

15. What should biblical worship look like today? (Psalm 100:4 - It needs to include listening to the Lord in His Word, receiving His grace through the Sacraments, remembering His sacrifice on the cross, and the washing of regeneration by His Spirit.
- There needs to be an opportunity for a response which includes giving thanks to God, praising Him, and praying to Him.
- Worship must include the fellowship of those who share a love for the Lord and a message of hope for those who don't yet know Him.)

9.   Prayer
Matthew 6:5-15

Matthew 6

[5]"And when you pray, do not be like the hypocrites, for they love to pray standing in the synagogues and on the street corners to be seen by men. I tell you the truth, they have received their reward in full. [6]But when you pray, go into your room, close the door and pray to your Father, who is unseen. Then your Father, who sees what is done in secret, will reward you. [7]And when you pray, do not keep on babbling like pagans, for they think they will be heard because of their many words. [8]Do not be like them, for your Father knows what you need before you ask him.

[9]"This, then, is how you should pray:

 " 'Our Father in heaven,
   hallowed be your name,
[10]your kingdom come,
   your will be done
      on earth as it is in heaven.
[11]Give us today our daily bread.
[12]Forgive us our debts,
      as we also have forgiven our debtors.
[13]And lead us not into temptation,
      but deliver us from the evil one. [14]For if you forgive men when they sin against you, your heavenly Father will also forgive you. [15]But if you do not forgive men their sins, your Father will not forgive your sins.

Study Questions: Prayer
Matthew 6:5-15

Introduction:
Prayer is an essential part of the believer's life. God commands us to pray and He promises to hear and answer when we pray (Matthew 7:7,8,11). Prayer serves as our communication link with God. Jesus taught His disciples how to pray and told them to address God as their Father. He wanted the disciples to understand the relationship that could exist between them and their Heavenly Father. Jesus invited them to pour out their hearts to God, even the small details.

Even though prayer is simply talking with God, we seem to forget to open our hearts and be honest with Him. Big words sound important, but the Lord is not looking for a show or for many convincing words. He just wants us to talk with Him as a son or daughter would talk to their father. Jesus gives us an example of this in the Lord's Prayer. In it He invites us to call His Father "our Father," and He Himself is the one that makes that relationship possible.

Grace Goals:
Knowledge
- To understand our need for prayer and relationship with God.
- To realize that we can come to God at any time and in any place to thank Him and bring our needs before Him!
- To recognize that God is both our Father as well as holy, that prayer is about His kingdom and His will and also our needs, our debts and our temptations.

Attitude
- To have faith that the Lord hears our prayers and will answer them according to His perfect will.
- To believe that God is able to do exceedingly more than we could ever ask or imagine.

Actions
- To daily meet Jesus in prayer and open our hearts to Him.
- To keep His name holy, confess our sins and seek His kingdom even as we make requests of the Lord.

Memory Verse:
2 Chronicles 7:14 "If my people, who are called by my name, will humble themselves and pray and seek my face and turn from their

wicked ways, then will I hear from heaven and will forgive their sin and will heal their land."

Questions about the Text:

1. What type of attitude is needed regarding prayer? (Mathew 6:5-8 We are not to be like the hypocrites praying for show, nor are we to be like the pagans, babbling with many words. We are to pray in humble trust in God because He is our Father and He knows our needs. Hebrews 11:6; James 4:1-3)

2. Why are we to go into our rooms and close the door as we pray? (Mathew 6:6-8 Because our Father, who is unseen, knows what we need. He will reward us according to His will and He desires a sincere relationship with His children. Romans 8:26-27)

3. What is the difference between the two rewards described? (Mathew 6:5-6 The hypocrites receive their reward by being seen by everyone. The one who prays unseen by others will receive his reward from his heavenly Father.)

4. What are the main topics covered in the Lord's Prayer that Jesus gives as an outline and guide for His disciples? (Mathew 6:9-13 The main topics are: hallowing the name of God, acknowledging His kingdom and will to be superior, our daily needs, forgiveness, and protection by the Lord for our lives.)

5. Why did Jesus teach His disciples to pray to God as Father? (Mathew 6:9 Through Jesus they were given the right to become children of God. It is Jesus' invitation and redemptive work that makes it possible.)

6. Why did Jesus tell the disciples to hallow God's name? (Mathew 6:9 To hallow God's name is to respect it and His whole being. To be holy means set apart and without sin. God's name and His whole character are holy, but in this prayer the disciples personally acknowledge His name as holy and they pray that His name would be honored among us.)

7. What does it mean that God's kingdom should come and His will be done? (Mathew 6:10 The kingdom of God comes when our heavenly Father gives us His Holy Spirit, so that by His grace we believe His holy Word and live a godly life here on

earth and in heaven forever.)

8. Why did Jesus teach them to say give us our daily bread? (Mathew 6:11 God is the provider of daily food and they were dependent on Him for it. He is also the one that supplies their every need. They were learning that everything is a gift from God. See Matthew 6:32-33.)

9. What did the disciples need to learn about the forgiveness of sin? (Mathew 6:12 They needed to remember that every sin is a sin against God. If He were to keep a record, the debt would be impossible to pay. In this prayer they ask God for His forgiveness and remember to forgive those who have done something against them. See Psalm 51:4.)

10. Why would they need to ask the Lord not to lead them into temptation? (Mathew 6:13 The Lord does not tempt anyone, but they acknowledge that they are tempted and they need the Lord's protection from Satan, the world and their own sinful nature, (James 1:13; 1 Corinthians 10:13). Jesus faced every temptation and defeated Satan at the cross and that is the only place for us to stand. See Hebrews 4:15-16.)

11. Why did Jesus give the warning about forgiving others? (Mathew 6:14-15 If they won't forgive others how could they expect the Lord to forgive them? Since every sin is against the Lord, the sins that others would commit against the disciples do not compare with their sins against the Lord.)

Application Questions:
1. What is prayer? ("Prayer is the childlike communion of our hearts with God in which we tell Him all our needs and earnestly seek some gift from Him." Sverdrup's Explanation to the Small Catechism "Ask and it will be given to you; seek and you will find; knock and the door will be opened to you." Matthew 7:7)

2. To whom do you look for strength and protection? Do you look to the Lord, or to those around you? (1 John 5:14-15; Psalm 18:2-3)

3. Do you take time to call upon the Lord in all circumstances, or just when you are having troubles? (1 Thessalonians 5:17; Luke 18:1-5; Jeremiah 33:3 ; Romans 8:26-27)

4. "When should we pray? (The attitude of our hearts should be one of constant prayer, and our communion with God should not be confined to certain times and places, but we should speak with Him whenever we feel need of it. See 1 Thessalonians 5:17 and Ephesians 6:18a)"

5. What precaution do we need to take when we pray? (Matthew 6:5-8 We need to confess our sin of pride, and seek humility from Him as we pray, not looking to draw attention to ourselves by the way we are praying. Rather we are to pray earnestly and come before God in reverence.)

6. With whom should we pray? (Matthew 6:6, Acts 12:5 We should spend time in prayer both alone with the Lord and with fellow believers.)

7. When is your personal prayer time?

8. What does it mean that God is our Father? (Matthew 6:9 He knows our needs, He listens to our prayers and He answers us when we seek Him. Calling Him Father we are able to understand a bit of the depths of His love and great care for us and the situation that we are in.)

9. How can we keep the Lord's name Holy? (Matthew 6:9 When we pray with humble respect. The way we speak to others about the Lord or how we use His name. If we are known as a Christian, how we live and what we say either honors or profanes the name of Jesus. We keep His name holy when we teach the Word of God in purity and keep it in our hearts." (question 283, Luther's Small Catechism Explained))

10. How does God's kingdom come to us, and when is His will done among us? (His kingdom comes to us through the Gospel Word of God, when we believe His Word and by faith become a part of His kingdom. The kingdom comes when the Gospel comes. This is His will for us.)

11. How do we acknowledge the Lord as provider of everything? (Matthew 6:11 We acknowledge Him when we thank Him in prayer and when we are thankful for what He gives us.)

12. How do we see the Lord allowing us to bring our needs and requests before Him? (Matthew 6:11 We see His love because He invites us to pray and desires to hear us. He provides for our every need.)

13. What are the temptations that we face? (Matthew 6:13 We all face the same temptations that are common to man. 1 John 2:16 says that they are the lust of the flesh, the lust of the eyes and the pride of life.)

14. Why it so important for us to daily forgive people who have sinned against us? (Matthew 6:14-15 Because sin is a barrier that will break down our relationship with God and with others. We are not judges, but the Lord is and He will judge everyone with justice. Refusal to forgive others indicates we do not believe He has truly forgiven us. Refusal to forgive others is a sign of unbelief.)

15. Is there any situation in prayer which is impossible for God to answer? Why? (Acts 12:6-12 No situation is too difficult for the Lord. He is all-powerful. He created the universe and everything in it. Ephesians 3:20; Matthew 21:20-22)

10. Salvation
Acts 16:23-34

Acts 16

²³After they had been severely flogged, they were thrown into prison, and the jailer was commanded to guard them carefully. ²⁴Upon receiving such orders, he put them in the inner cell and fastened their feet in the stocks.

²⁵About midnight Paul and Silas were praying and singing hymns to God, and the other prisoners were listening to them. ²⁶Suddenly there was such a violent earthquake that the foundations of the prison were shaken. At once all the prison doors flew open, and everybody's chains came loose. ²⁷The jailer woke up, and when he saw the prison doors open, he drew his sword and was about to kill himself because he thought the prisoners had escaped. ²⁸But Paul shouted, "Don't harm yourself! We are all here!"

²⁹The jailer called for lights, rushed in and fell trembling before Paul and Silas. ³⁰He then brought them out and asked, "Sirs, what must I do to be saved?"

³¹They replied, "Believe in the Lord Jesus, and you will be saved—you and your household." ³²Then they spoke the word of the Lord to him and to all the others in his house. ³³At that hour of the night the jailer took them and washed their wounds; then immediately he and all his family were baptized. ³⁴The jailer brought them into his house and set a meal before them; he was filled with joy because he had come to believe in God—he and his whole family.

Study Questions: Salvation
Acts 16:23-34

Introduction:
Christ's body, the church, needs to have a personal relationship with Jesus the head of the church. We also need to offer salvation to the hurting and lost world around us. The church consists of believers who seek salvation for themselves and for others through the Word of God and the sacraments that He has given us.

On their missionary journey, Paul and Silas stopped at many cities proclaiming the Good News of Jesus Christ for the salvation of all who would believe in Him. Even though many believed, others were angered and upset by the fact that the message of Jesus was for both the Jews and the Gentiles. On one journey, in Philippi, Paul commanded a demon to leave a girl. As a result Paul and Silas were severely beaten and thrown into prison. However, even in prison, Paul and Silas found a way to make the message of Jesus Christ known.

Grace Goals:
Knowledge
- To understand that there is only one way to be saved, and that is through believing in the Son of God: Jesus Christ.
- To learn that salvation is for everyone, young and old alike.
- To learn that all mankind is unworthy of the Gospel but that that salvation is in fact by grace.

Attitude
- To find peace and joy in Jesus regardless of the situation.
- To marvel at the way God uses situations.

Actions
- To repent and believe and be saved.
- To watch for opportunities to share Jesus with people the Lord brings us into contact with.
- To bring our whole family to the Lord.

Memory Verse:
Colossians 2:14-14, "When you were dead in your sins and in the uncircumcision of your sinful nature, God made you alive with Christ. He forgave us all our sins, having canceled the written code, with its regulations, that was against us and that stood opposed to us; He took it away, nailing it to the cross."

63

Questions about the Text:

1. Why were Paul and Silas beaten and thrown into prison? (Acts 16:23 They had been telling people how they could be saved and had cast a demon out of a slave girl who made her owners a great deal of money by fortune telling.)

2. What is interesting about the harsh treatment used against Paul and Silas? (Acts 16:23-24 They were not doing anything that would merit harsh treatment nor were they a threat to anyone that that would cause a need for a guard.)

3. What does the attitude and response of Paul and Silas say about them? (Acts 16:25 They responded with kindness though they had been treated harshly. They were trusting in God, praying and singing hymns to God in spite of how they had been treated. It showed their confident faith in God and the importance of the message. Matthew 5:11-12; 5:43-44)

4. What is significant about Paul and Silas' time in prison? (Acts 16:25-26 After being severely flogged they sang songs and prayed to God and the other prisoners were listening to them. There was a violent earthquake, the doors flew open and all of the prisoners' chains came loose, but they stayed in prison!)

5. Why did the jailer decide to kill himself when he was awakened by the earthquake? (Acts 16:27 He thought that the prisoners had escaped and he was accountable for them.)

6. Why did Paul call out to him, "Don't harm yourself! We are all here!"? (Acts 16:28 He had compassion on the jailer, even though they had been treated so harshly.)

7. Why did the jailer come to Paul and Silas trembling and asking how he could be saved? (Acts 16:29-30 He came face to face with a power that was greater than beatings, chains and even prison itself. He could see that he and his whole family needed what Paul and Silas had.)

8. What does the statement "Believe in the Lord Jesus, and you will be saved" mean? (Acts 16:31 It means to be saved from God's wrath, Romans 5:9, from death, Romans 5:20-21, and from slavery to sin. Romans 6:14, 17-18)

9. What did Paul and Silas then do for the jailer and what did the jailer do for them? (Acts 16:32-33 Paul and Silas spoke the Word of the Lord to him and baptized his whole family. The jailer washed their wounds, took them into his house and set a meal before them.)

10. What gave the jailer great joy? (Acts 16:34 He and his whole family had come to believe in God.)

Application Questions:
1. How do we see that following Christ in our own lives is not always easy, and often may be difficult or painful? (Acts 16:23-24 When we follow Christ, we will face mocking, persecution, pain and suffering. 2 Timothy 1:8-9; 3:12)

2. What possible responses are before us when we are faced with pain, suffering, and hardships? (Acts 16:25 We can respond in anger, bitterness and revenge, or we can show what faith in God looks like to a watching world. We can turn to the Lord in prayer, since we know that He is in control and we can continue to praise and glorify Him in every situation.)

3. How can we, like Paul and Silas, witness for Jesus Christ wherever we are? (Acts 16:25 In any circumstance, we can point the people around us to Jesus by our words and actions. These both are part of our testimony.)

4. What is life like for people who are not following Jesus as their Lord and Savior? (Acts 16:27 There is fear. Life may not seem worth living and as a result, it may seem easier to die than to face life.)

5. What can we offer people who are lost, hopeless, and confused in their thinking? (Acts 16:28 We can reach out to them in love, warn them of the danger they are in and share with them the hope that surpasses the trials. Romans 3:20-26)

6. Why is it important to be prepared to share the message of salvation with people who are spiritually lost? (Acts 16:29-30 We don't know when the Holy Spirit is working in someone's heart or when they will ask us how to be saved. We must be ready to lead them to Jesus. See Acts 4:12)

7. How is an individual saved? (Acts 16:31 We must call them to believe in the Lord Jesus Christ and call on His name for salvation. Romans 10:8-13; Ephesians 2:1-10. Remind them that their salvation is not based upon their prayer or any work that they have done but by the completed work of Christ on the cross.)

8. What else is required to bring salvation to an unbeliever, as illustrated in this story? (Acts 16:32-33 Speaking the Word of God and offering them new life. They were baptized into their new faith immediately. Titus 3:3-7. Apart from this we also see the importance of the Holy Spirit teaching one to know Christ in a true and living faith. Romans 8:9, 14)

9. What do we learn from this story about who can be saved? (Acts 16:34 We learn that salvation is for all who believe. It can be for young or old, individuals or for a family. It is for all people. 1 Timothy 2:3-4; Mark 16:15-16)

10. What does salvation by faith in Jesus Christ bring to the person who receives it? (Acts 16:34 Salvation in Jesus Christ brings great joy to the person whose life has been changed.)

11. Baptism
Acts 2:22-41

Acts 2

²²"Men of Israel, listen to this: Jesus of Nazareth was a man accredited by God to you by miracles, wonders and signs, which God did among you through him, as you yourselves know. ²³This man was handed over to you by God's set purpose and foreknowledge; and you, with the help of wicked men, put him to death by nailing him to the cross. ²⁴But God raised him from the dead, freeing him from the agony of death, because it was impossible for death to keep its hold on him. ²⁵David said about him:

" 'I saw the Lord always before me.
Because he is at my right hand,
I will not be shaken.
²⁶Therefore my heart is glad and my tongue rejoices;
my body also will live in hope,
²⁷because you will not abandon me to the grave,
nor will you let your Holy One see decay.
²⁸You have made known to me the paths of life;
you will fill me with joy in your presence.'

²⁹"Brothers, I can tell you confidently that the patriarch David died and was buried, and his tomb is here to this day. ³⁰But he was a prophet and knew that God had promised him on oath that he would place one of his descendants on his throne. ³¹Seeing what was ahead, he spoke of the resurrection of the Christ, that He was not abandoned to the grave, nor did his body see decay. ³²God has raised this Jesus to life, and we are all witnesses of the fact. ³³Exalted to the right hand of God, he has received from the Father the promised Holy Spirit and has poured out what you now see and hear. ³⁴For David did not ascend to heaven, and yet he said,

"'The Lord said to my Lord: "Sit at my right hand
³⁵until I make your enemies a footstool for your feet."

³⁶"Therefore let all Israel be assured of this: God has made this Jesus, whom you crucified, both Lord and Christ."

³⁷When the people heard this, they were cut to the heart and said to Peter and the other apostles, "Brothers, what shall we do?"

³⁸Peter replied, "Repent and be baptized, every one of you, in the name of Jesus Christ for the forgiveness of your sins. And you will receive the gift of the Holy Spirit. ³⁹The promise is for you and your children and for all who are far off—for all whom the Lord our God will call."

67

[40]With many other words he warned them; and he pleaded with them, "Save yourselves from this corrupt generation." [41]Those who accepted his message were baptized, and about three thousand were added to their number that day.

Study Questions: Baptism
Acts 2:22-41

Introduction:
After Jesus had risen from the dead and had spent 40 days with His disciples, He ascended into heaven with the promise that He was sending the Holy Spirit to them. After the disciples spent time in Jerusalem waiting, the Holy Spirit came upon them in tongues of fire and they spoke with boldness the good news of Jesus. The Holy Spirit was going before the disciples, not just being with them but also now dwelling in them. At this time, there were many people gathered from across the nations. Peter stood in front of a large crowd of people and explained to them who Jesus Christ is, and how to be saved.

Peter offered the people a gift. It was a gift of forgiveness of their sins, it was the gift of the Holy Spirit, and it was the promise of God for individuals, for children, and for all who were far off. It was a gift made available through the call of God and the sacrifice of Jesus. That gift was available to everyone who repented and was baptized.

Grace Goals:
> Knowledge
> – To understand the promise and provision of baptism.
> – To acknowledge that we are raised to new life through baptism.
>
> Attitude
> – To gladly welcome the Holy Spirit into our lives.
> – To be convicted of our sin.
>
> Actions
> – To preach the good news of Jesus Christ to people around us, teaching them and baptizing them.
> – To obey Jesus wholeheartedly and live by the power of the Holy Spirit at work in us.

Memory Verse:
> 1 Peter 3:21 "And this water symbolizes baptism that now saves you also—not the removal of dirt from the body but the pledge of a good conscience toward God. It saves you by the resurrection of

Questions about the Text:

1. What was Peter trying to point out about Jesus? (Acts 2:22-24 Peter was pointing out that they had killed Jesus and that they were as guilty of His death as the ones that had nailed Him to the cross. Even still, God raised Him from the dead, for it was impossible for death to keep its hold on Jesus.)

2. Why is it important for the crowd to see their connection with Jesus' death? (Acts 2:23 It was essential for them to see their own sin and guilt or they would not see their need for forgiveness and new life.)

3. Why did Peter bring up King David's quote from Psalm 16? (Acts 2:25-28 David was prophesying about his Lord and the promised life beyond the grave. David died and was abandoned to the grave. The promised Holy One would be raised to life. He would be the path of life and would not be abandoned to the grave.)

4. How can Peter make such bold statements about the resurrection of the Christ, that He was not abandoned to the grave, His body did not see decay and that God raised Jesus to life? (Acts 2:31-32 The crucifixion and resurrection had only taken place 50 days earlier and these people were truly witnesses of it all.)

5. What is the point of restating that the people of Israel crucified Jesus, but God made him Lord and Christ? (Acts 2:36 It pointed out the people's sin and their need for forgiveness and it shows the power of God over death along with the fact that Jesus is in fact alive.)

6. What is the reaction to the presentation of Peter's message? (Acts 2:37 The people were convicted of their sin and responded by wanting to know what they should do.)

7. What is the evidence of the Holy Spirit's work in their life? (Acts 2:37 They were cut to the heart and asked what they must do.)

8. Why did Peter tell them to repent and be baptized? (Acts 2:38 So they could be forgiven of their sin and so they could receive the gift of the Holy Spirit. See also Acts 22:16)

9. In what way did Peter say the people should be baptized? (Acts 2:38 In the name of Jesus Christ. See also Matthew 28:19-20; Mark 16:16)

10. Who did Peter say this promise was for? (Acts 2:39 He said it was for every one of them, including children and those that were far off, because it was a promise for all whom the Lord God would call to Himself. Acts 16:33; Matthew 18:1-6; 19:13-15; Colossians 2:11-12 where baptism is compared to circumcision.)

11. What was the result of Peter's message? (Acts 2:40-41 Three thousand people accepted his message. They were baptized, added to the number of believers and were saved.)

Application Questions:
1. Who killed Jesus? Was it the crowd that Peter challenged, was it those who nailed Him to the cross, or are we responsible since He died for our sins?

2. Why is it important that we see our own sin? (Acts 2:22-24 Every person must see their sin before they will see or understand their need for a Savior.)

3. What difference does Jesus' resurrection from the dead make for us? (Acts 2:24, 31-32 The resurrection is the fulfillment of prophecy, the evidence of God's power and hope for the future. In life... we die, but in baptism... we are raised to new life in Christ. By the resurrection Jesus was declared with power to be the Son of God. Romans 1:4)

4. How can we be certain that the message we preach is true? (Acts 2:32 There were many witnesses in Bible times that Jesus Christ was raised from the dead and is alive now. The God who cannot lie guarantees the truth of the message preached.)

5. We know that God was able to raise Jesus from the dead and make Him both Lord and Christ. What does this tell us about His power to save us? (Acts 2:32, 36 God is able to make us new creations in Jesus Christ. He claims us as His own and gives us eternal life.)

71

6. How should we instruct people who are under conviction for their sins? (Acts 2:38 We should invite them to repent of their sins, be united with Christ and to be baptized. Ezekiel 36:24-26 points out God's work on our behalf.)

7. Should we forbid anyone from repentance and being united with Christ? (Acts 2:38 No, this gift is for everyone, both young and old and all whom the Lord would call. See also Matthew 18:1-4)

8. When we baptize people in the name of Jesus Christ, what happens to them? (Acts 2:38 They are united with Him in death, and they are raised with Him in life. They receive forgiveness of sins and the gift of the Holy Spirit. See also 1 Peter 3:21; Galatians 3:26-27; Romans 6:3-4; Titus 3:4-7)

9. What is baptism? (Baptism is not simply water, but it is the water used according to God's command and connected with God's Word.)

10. In whose name then are you baptized? (I am baptized in the name of the Father and of the Son and of the Holy Spirit. Matthew 28:19. In Baptism I have entered into fellowship with the Triune God- the Father, the Son, and the Holy Spirit; I have become His own and have been made heir of all His gracious gifts. Colossians 2:12.)

11. How should we baptize people? (The Bible uses many modes in which water was used. In the water along the way, Acts 8:36-38; plenty of water, John 3:23; sprinkling with water, Ezekiel 36:25; with the water at hand, Acts 16:33)

12. Who should administer Baptism? (Baptism should be administered by the minister of the congregation, but when necessary it may be administered by any Christian. 1 Corinthians 14:40.)

13. How can water do such great things? (Luther's Small Catechism states, "It is not the water, indeed, that does such great things, but the Word of God, connected with the water, and our faith which relies on that Word of God. For without the Word of God, it is simply water and no baptism. But when connected with the Word of God, it is a baptism, that is, a

gracious water of life and a washing of regeneration in the Holy Spirit, as St. Paul says to Titus, in the third chapter: 'He saved us, not on the basis of deeds which we have done in righteousness, but according to His mercy, by the washing of regeneration and renewing by the Holy Spirit, whom He poured out upon us richly through Jesus Christ our Savior; so that being justified by His grace we would be made heirs according to the hope of eternal life. This is a trustworthy statement.'")

14. What benefit do we have from Baptism? (Baptism works the forgiveness of sins, delivers from death and the devil, and gives everlasting salvation to all who believe, as the Word and promise of God declares. See Acts 2:38, 22:16; Romans 6:4; Galatians 3:27; Colossians 2:12; Titus 3:5; 1 Peter 3:21.)

15. How is our generation corrupt and how can we be saved from it? (Acts 2:39 Our generation, like Peter's, has done the same thing to Jesus as before. We also must repent and be baptized in the name of Jesus Christ for forgiveness.)

12. Lord's Supper
1 Corinthians 11:20-30

1 Corinthians 11

[20]When you come together, it is not the Lord's Supper you eat, [21]for as you eat, each of you goes ahead without waiting for anybody else. One remains hungry, another gets drunk. [22]Don't you have homes to eat and drink in? Or do you despise the church of God and humiliate those who have nothing? What shall I say to you? Shall I praise you for this? Certainly not!

[23]For I received from the Lord what I also passed on to you: The Lord Jesus, on the night he was betrayed, took bread, [24]and when he had given thanks, he broke it and said, "This is my body, which is for you; do this in remembrance of me." [25]In the same way, after supper he took the cup, saying, "This cup is the new covenant in my blood; do this, whenever you drink it, in remembrance of me." [26]For whenever you eat this bread and drink this cup, you proclaim the Lord's death until he comes.

[27]Therefore, whoever eats the bread or drinks the cup of the Lord in an unworthy manner will be guilty of sinning against the body and blood of the Lord. [28]A man ought to examine himself before he eats of the bread and drinks of the cup. [29]For anyone who eats and drinks without recognizing the body of the Lord eats and drinks judgment on himself. [30]That is why many among you are weak and sick, and a number of you have fallen asleep.

Study Questions: Lord's Supper
1 Corinthians 11:20-30

Introduction:
On the night that He was betrayed, the Lord Jesus Christ instituted the sacrament of the Lord's Supper, Holy Communion, and this meal parallels the Passover meal in Egypt when the blood of the lamb was put on the door to save the first born from the angel of death. When believers take communion, they partake of the real presence of the body and blood of Christ assuring them that they are saved from the death of sin. Jesus told His disciples to practice this sacrament in remembrance of Him.

This instruction from Jesus was not only for the disciples, but also for the spiritual nourishment of believers today. This sacrament is different than the sacrament of baptism in that we are urged to examine ourselves before partaking in it. This is so that we will realize the sin of our own lives and think seriously about the price that was paid for our forgiveness, even though we are unworthy. The blood that Jesus shed for us is what makes us acceptable to God.

Grace Goals:
Knowledge
- To understand the sacrament of the Lord's Supper and its role in the believer's life.
- To remember the parallel meal and sacrifice that was offered at Passover in Egypt to save the firstborn children.

Attitude
- To believe that Jesus Christ is Himself present with us, as we take the bread and wine.
- To strengthen, renew, and restore us as we remember the price He paid for our sins when He died on the cross.

Actions
- To celebrate the Lord's Supper with other believers remembering what Christ has done for us and rejoicing that our sins are in fact paid in full.

Memory Verse:
1 Corinthians 10:16 "Is not the cup of thanksgiving for which we give thanks a participation in the blood of Christ? And is not the bread that we break a participation in the body of Christ?"

Questions about the Text:

1. What was Paul's main concern for the believers in Corinth as they took the Lord's Supper? (1 Corinthians 11:21 They were not showing respect to this holy meal that the Lord had instituted. They were indulging in the food as if it were just food and they did not give consideration to the others.)

2. When did the Lord Jesus establish the Lord's Supper? (1 Corinthians 11:23 On the night in which He was betrayed, which was His Passover celebration on the night before His crucifixion. Matthew 26:26-29; Mark 14:12-26; Luke 22:19-23; John 6:53-58)

3. What are the physical elements of the Lord's Supper that Jesus used? (1 Corinthians 11:23, 25 Bread and fruit of the vine, the cup.)

4. Why did Jesus say, "This is my body" as He broke the bread? (1 Corinthians 11:24 The bread was not only bread, but it was His body because of His word. 1 Corinthians 10:14-17; Matthew 26:16-18)

5. Why did Jesus say, "This cup is the new covenant in My blood." as He took the cup? (1 Corinthians 11:25 The old covenant of animal blood sacrifices was now fulfilled in the perfect sacrifice of Jesus once and for all. See also Hebrews 9:18-28)

6. What does He mean by saying, "Do this in remembrance of me?" (1 Corinthians 11:24-25 The instruction is to remember the sacrifice made and the price paid for our sin.)

7. Who did Christ say was to receive both His body and blood? (1 Corinthians 11:24-25 "You," which is first directed to the disciples who were with Him, and then all believers who would follow Him. Matthew 26:27-28)

8. Until Christ's return, how do believers proclaim the Lord's death when they eat of the bread and drink of the cup? (1 Corinthians 11:26 They remember what Jesus did and the forgiveness that is ours.)

9. What are the dangers when believers partake of the Lord's Supper? (1 Corinthians 11:27 They can take it in an unworthy manner. They can sin by dishonoring the body and blood of the Lord. They can eat and drink judgment on themselves. 1 Corinthians 10:21)

10. What does it mean to not recognize the body of Christ? (1 Corinthians 11:29 It means to take the bread and wine casually, not considering our partnership with Him. 1 Corinthians 10:15-16)

11. What must a person do before he eats of the bread and drinks of the cup? (1 Corinthians 11:28 He must examine himself and ask forgiveness for his sin. Psalm 139:23-24)

12. What is the parallel between the Passover meal and this Lord's Supper? (1 Corinthians 11:26-29 In the Passover meal the sacrifice is what saved the first born from the death angel, so also in this meal it is the sacrifice of Jesus that saves us from the death of sin. See also 1 Peter 2:24)

Application Questions:
1. How can we show respect when we take the Lord's Supper? (1 Corinthians 11:21 We can take the Lord's Supper with a holy reverence for the gift given, the sacrifice made and the price paid for our sins.)

2. What is important about the timing Jesus chose when He established the Lord's Supper on the night of His betrayal? (1 Corinthians 11:23 By teaching it on the night He was betrayed, Jesus showed us the extent of His forgiveness. Even to the very one who would turn against Him.)

3. What value do the bread and wine have for us as believers? (1 Corinthians 11:23-25 They are physical elements that remind us in a tangible way that the Lord Jesus died for our sins. The Lord's Supper unites the believer with food and drink to Christ Himself.)

4. How can taking part in the Lord's Supper actually give us the forgiveness of sins? Is not forgiveness of sins only found in the finished work of Christ? ("The eating and drinking, indeed, do not produce them, but the words: "Given and shed for you for the forgiveness of sins." For besides the bodily

eating and drinking, these words are the chief thing in the Sacrament; and anyone who believes them has what they say and declare, namely, the forgiveness of sins." And yes, it is true that apart from Christ's finished work there is no forgiveness of sins but God in His great mercy has tied His love and grace to external means so that we are able to hear, taste, feel and smell the promises that our sins are indeed paid in full!)

5. Why do we as followers of Christ believe that the bread and wine are in fact the body and blood of Jesus? (1 Corinthians 11:23-25 We as followers believe this because Christ plainly stated: "This is my body," and "This is my blood." So we take Christ at His Word.)

6. How often are we supposed to celebrate the Lord's Supper in remembrance of Jesus? (1 Corinthians 11:23-25 We should not take the Lord's Supper only once, but rather we should do this frequently to help us remember what Christ did for us. According to Scripture there is not schedule given of how often we are to partake.)

7. Why is it important for older believers to instruct younger believers about what the Lord's Supper truly is? (1 Corinthians 11:27 It is very important to carefully teach younger believers, because taking the Lord's Supper in an unworthy manner is sin and brings judgment.)

8. What does it mean to examine oneself? (1 Corinthians 11:28 When a believer examines himself before taking communion, he realizes that he is a sinner and desperately needs the forgiveness through the body and blood of Jesus for renewal, restoration, and unity with Christ.)

9. Who should participate in the Lord's Supper? (1 Corinthians 11:23-29 The celebration of the Lord's Supper is for every believer who has rightly examined himself. The practice is reserved for those who can fully understand their sin and who can truly examine themselves.)

10. Who then truly takes part of the Lord's Supper in a worthy manner? (Fasting and bodily preparation are good outward discipline, but the person is prepared who believe the words: "Given and shed for you for the forgiveness of sins." But

anyone who does not believe these words or who doubts them is not prepared, for the words "for you" require truly believing hearts.)

11. What should be served in the Lord's Supper? (1 Corinthians 11:23-25; See also Matthew 26:26-29 Just as Christ instituted the Lord's Supper using bread and the cup of the fruit of the vine, so believers should celebrate this sacrament using such elements in the practice of the sacrament.)

12. What manner of style or practices do people use today?

Promises of Forgiveness:

Isaiah 1:18	Isaiah 53:5	1 John 1:8-9
Psalm 103:11-12	Ephesians 1:7	Psalm 32:1-2
Psalm 130:3-4	Romans 8:1	

Church

Lessons 13-25

13. Church Foundation
Matthew 16:15-19 & 1 Peter 2:4-9

Matthew 16

15 "But what about you?" he asked. "Who do you say I am?"

16 Simon Peter answered, "You are the Christ, the Son of the living God."

17 Jesus replied, "Blessed are you, Simon son of Jonah, for this was not revealed to you by man, but by my Father in heaven.

18 And I tell you that you are Peter, and on this rock I will build my church, and the gates of Hades will not overcome it.

19 I will give you the keys of the kingdom of heaven; whatever you bind on earth will be bound in heaven, and whatever you loose on earth will be loosed in heaven."

1 Peter 2

4 As you come to him, the living Stone-- rejected by men but chosen by God and precious to him--

5 you also, like living stones, are being built into a spiritual house to be a holy priesthood, offering spiritual sacrifices acceptable to God through Jesus Christ.

6 For in Scripture it says: "See, I lay a stone in Zion, a chosen and precious cornerstone, and the one who trusts in him will never be put to shame."

7 Now to you who believe, this stone is precious. But to those who do not believe, "The stone the builders rejected has become the capstone,"

8 and, "A stone that causes men to stumble and a rock that makes them fall." They stumble because they disobey the message-- which is also what they were destined for.

9 But you are a chosen people, a royal priesthood, a holy nation, a people belonging to God, that you may declare the praises of him who called you out of darkness into his wonderful light.

Study Questions: Church Foundation
Matthew 16:15-19 & 1 Peter 2:4-9

Introduction:

The word church means "called out" or "the called out ones." The church is made up of the people who are called out of the world and have made God their king. It is described as the body of Christ, the bride of Christ, the house of God, and a holy place. It is the place where Jesus reigns on earth, His kingdom on earth. The congregation is the right form of the kingdom of God on earth.

In this text Peter makes a parallel between the physical church building and the living church made up of those who believe in Christ. It is astonishing to consider the description of this Church, the honor that it is given and its role in God's plan. It does not describe ranks or roles of people, everyone who believes is a part of this holy community built on the one foundation of Jesus Himself. It is a privileged position that the Lord alone can grant.

Grace Goals:

Knowledge
- To recognize the foundation of the church is faith.
- To understand that the church of God is made up of all believers in Jesus.
- To know that we have a high calling as people of God.

Attitude
- To have confidence in that Jesus will build His church
- To believe that we are indeed a chosen people, a royal priesthood, a holy nation, and a people belonging to God.

Actions
- To declare God's praises to a dark world and storm hell's gates.
- To partner with those who are also part of God's kingdom.

Memory Verse:

Ephesians 1:22-23, "And God placed all things under his feet and appointed him to be head over everything for the church, which is his body, the fullness of him who fills everything in every way."

Questions about the Text:
Matthew 16

1. What is the rock that Jesus will build His church on? (Matthew 16:16; It is Peter's declaration of who Jesus is. It is Peter's foundation of faith rather than he himself as a person. Ephesians 1:22-23 says, "And God placed all things under [Jesus] feet and appointed him to be head over everything for the church, which is his body, the fullness of him who fills everything in every way.")

2. How are people separated by their definition of Jesus? (Matthew 16:15-16; It separates believers from unbelievers. Peter's response was one of faith. It separates those who look to Scripture and the fulfilled prophecy for a Messiah versus those who do not know who Jesus is. It separates those that are trusting the living God verses an unknown God.)

3. What is this blessing of God that Simon is given? (Matthew 16:17; He is given the blessing of the revelation from God to know who Jesus is. He is given the blessing of the gift of faith to be able to say who Jesus is.)

4. How does Jesus change Peter's destination? (Matthew 16:18; Peter was given the Kingdom of heaven, the gates of hell do not have power over him.)

1 Peter

5. Who is this living Stone and why is He described like that? (1 Peter 2:4, 7 The living Stone is Jesus. He is the one that was rejected by men but chosen by God. He is the precious cornerstone. He is the foundation of faith, He is the head of the church. And He is the one that gives it life. See also 1 Corinthians 3:11)

6. How does the church come to Him? (1 Peter 2:4-5, 7 Instead of rejecting Him they accept Him. Verse 7 says clearly that it those who believe.)

7. Why is the church described as living stones? (1 Peter 2:5 Jesus the living Stone can only live in those who are also alive. Jesus Himself is the one that makes dead stones live. Only these living stones can be built into a spiritual house, can be a holy priesthood, or can offer spiritual sacrifices.)

8. What is this spiritual house or holy priesthood? (1 Peter 2:5 The people of God are that house, they are the those priests. They are the home where the Spirit of God lives. They are set apart for the Lord and His sacrifices. His people are made acceptable to God through Jesus Christ alone.)

9. What does trusting in him mean? (1 Peter 2:6-7 It is more than an intellectual belief, it is a surrender of ones earthly life and a trust of one's eternal destination. This trust will not fail because the one in whom the trust is given is faithful.)

10. How does this stone cause them to stumble or fall? (1 Peter 2:7-8 It causes them to fall because they have rejected Jesus the stone that became the capstone. They stumble because they disobey the message that salvation is through trust in him. This scripture comes from Psalm 118:22 and is quoted seven times in the New Testament referring to Jesus.)

11. What importance does verse 9 have for Christ's church? (1 Peter 2:9 The first four statements are actions that God has done and do not depend on anything about His people. He is the one that chose them, makes them royal, sets them apart, and claims them as His own. He is even the one that called them out of darkness into His light. The only role that His people play is declaring His praises.)

Application Questions:
Matthew 16

1. What is the foundation of the Christian church? (Matthew 16:16; The church is built on faith in Jesus. He is a solid foundation to build the church on because He is completely righteous and our hope is based on his righteousness.)

2. Who do people see Jesus as today? (People see Him as a good person, a prophet, or one of the gods. Christians see Him as the Son of the Living God.)

3. How does God's blessing come to us today? (We have His clear infallible Word. We can know God and have a relationship with him.)

4. What difference can knowing our destination make for us? (We have anticipation, even longing for heaven, and we have no fear of hell but a sweet peace.)

5. If Jesus is the living Stone, what difference does that make for us today? (1 Peter 2:4, 7 He is the foundation of the church, the cornerstone of our faith. He is our solid foundation, who gives us physical and spiritual life.

6. How do we accept or reject Him? (1 Peter 2:4-5, 7 We reject Him when we try to reach God on our own efforts rather than by Jesus' sacrifice on the cross. We reject Him when we think that we are good enough in ourselves rather than in Christ alone. We accept Him when we humbly cry out to Jesus for the forgiveness of our sins.)

7. What does a church full of living stones look like? (1 Peter 2:5 It is a church that is spiritually alive. The presence of Jesus can be seen as people leave their lives of sin. They do not look like the world but they care for the people in the world. The sacrifices that they make are done joyfully as unto the Lord.)

8. What is our role as a church to be? (1 Peter 2:5 The church must be a place where, the Word of God is communicated clearly, the sacraments are shared, the Lord is worshiped, sins are forgiven, and we serve one another.)

9. Is everyone that gathers in the physical church building a Christian? (1 Peter 2:6-7 No, there are some that believe in Jesus as their Savior and others that reject the living Stone. Some may outwardly confess Jesus but inwardly deny Him with their lives.)

10. What causes people to stumble or fall in their faith? (1 Peter 2:7-8 People try to please God with their good works rather than putting their trust in Christ. Other people want to continue in a self-centered life of sin. Still others struggle to trust in Jesus because they see hypocrisy in the church and they equate sinful men with their view of Jesus. There are many reasons people stumble in their faith.)

11. Why do we need to hear God's declaration in verse 9? (1 Peter 2:9 We need to know that the Lord has chosen us to be His people. We are loved. We need to know that we are royalty because He is the King and we are invited to be His

children. We are holy because He has set us apart and has forgiven us. We need to know that we belong to God and we are accepted because of Jesus. These facts produce praise.)

14. Church Invisible
Acts 8:9-25

Acts 8

9 Now for some time a man named Simon had practiced sorcery in the city and amazed all the people of Samaria. He boasted that he was someone great, 10 and all the people, both high and low, gave him their attention and exclaimed, "This man is the divine power known as the Great Power."

11 They followed him because he had amazed them for a long time with his magic.

12 But when they believed Philip as he preached the good news of the kingdom of God and the name of Jesus Christ, they were baptized, both men and women.

13 Simon himself believed and was baptized. And he followed Philip everywhere, astonished by the great signs and miracles he saw.

14 When the apostles in Jerusalem heard that Samaria had accepted the word of God, they sent Peter and John to them.

15 When they arrived, they prayed for them that they might receive the Holy Spirit,

16 because the Holy Spirit had not yet come upon any of them; they had simply been baptized into the name of the Lord Jesus.

17 Then Peter and John placed their hands on them, and they received the Holy Spirit.

18 When Simon saw that the Spirit was given at the laying on of the apostles' hands, he offered them money

19 and said, "Give me also this ability so that everyone on whom I lay my hands may receive the Holy Spirit."

20 Peter answered: "May your money perish with you, because you thought you could buy the gift of God with money!

21 You have no part or share in this ministry, because your heart is not right before God.

22 Repent of this wickedness and pray to the Lord. Perhaps he will forgive you for having such a thought in your heart.

23 For I see that you are full of bitterness and captive to sin."

24 Then Simon answered, "Pray to the Lord for me so that nothing you have said may happen to me."

25 When they had testified and proclaimed the word of the Lord, Peter and John returned to Jerusalem, preaching the gospel in many Samaritan villages.

Study Questions: Church Invisible
Acts 8:9-25

Introduction:

Church buildings are easy to see, but the kingdom of God is not encircled by walls. The work of God is often unseen, it takes place in the unseen areas of people's hearts, but the results of that work can be very evident in the lives of people who trust in Jesus. Not all people who attend churches are believers. They need salvation like Simon in this text.

In the people that gather to worship, there are some who sincerely trust the Lord but struggle to live out their faith. There are others who outwardly look like believers, but inwardly their hearts are far from the Lord. The harsh word of God's judgment causes people to flee to the Lord for mercy. The good news of the kingdom of God creates faith in the Lord Jesus. Both the Law of God and the good news of Jesus are needed for the invisible Church who make up the congregation of believers.

Grace Goals:
>   Knowledge
> - To understand that there is an invisible kingdom of God that includes those that are trusting in Jesus.
> - To understand that there is a visible gathering of believers that we call the church with both believers and unbelievers.

>   Attitude
> - To be humble before others rather than judgmental over them.
> - To realize that our hearts, like Simon, need correction.

>   Actions
> - To welcome everyone into the church to hear the word.
> - To be active participants of the kingdom of God.

Questions about the Text:
1. What makes someone great? (Acts 8:9-10 Simon had amazed the people and they had given him their attention and praise, but these are only outward responses. Greatness must be defined by one who is greater, not one that is lesser. Simon boasted about being great, but he saw something greater in Philip. Philip's greatness came from the good news of the kingdom of God and the name of Jesus.)

2. Why was Simon not the divine power or the Great Power? (Acts 8:10 There is only one divine power. Simon was simply a man who had fooled those under his influence. Jesus is divine, He is the Great Power.)

3. What is magic? (Acts 8:11 Magic uses quick hands to hide things from those that are watching. What is seen is not always what is real because those watching have been fooled. Witchcraft uses demonic influences to affect people or things.)

4. What is the kingdom of God? (Acts 8:12 The kingdom of God is wherever God is King. He rules over all of creation and yet a person can resist His rule over their heart. God's rule over the heart of man happens through the preaching of the good news of the kingdom of God in the name of the Lord Jesus Christ. The effect of the Lord's work on people's lives includes repentance from sin, crying out for the Lord's mercy, and baptism, which He alone can do.)

5. Why were the people being baptized? (Acts 8:12 They were hearing the good news of the kingdom of God, salvation in the name of Jesus, and forgiveness of sins. In baptism they were brought into the kingdom of God. They left the past, were cleansed from sin, and made a new creation.)

6. Why was Simon baptized? (Acts 8:13 It says that Simon believed but it also says that he was "astonished by the great signs and miracles he saw.")

7. Why is important that they sent Peter and John to Samaria? (Acts 8:14-17 The apostles were sent to each new place where people were accepting the Word of God. Their presence **confirmed** the message that Philip had shared and their prayer for the Holy Spirit **completed** the work of God in these new believers' lives.)

8. What is the connection between baptism and the Holy Spirit? (Acts 8:15 It says that they were "baptized into the name of the Lord Jesus" and they received the Holy Spirit. The Holy Spirit is a "gift of God" given by the Lord at baptism. These believers did not do anything to receive that gift other than to be baptized. This shows that baptism of the Holy Spirit and water baptism are not two separate events but beginning with

Pentecost, water baptism and the baptism of the Holy Spirit are actually one event and gift.)

9. Why did Simon offer the apostles money? (Acts 8:18 Simon was still caught in his former way of thinking where he controlled people and amazed them with his powers. He was still thinking from the perspective of the kingdom of man rather than from the kingdom of God.)

10. What does Peter's reply mean? (Acts 8:20-21 Simon's outward actions were correct, but his heart was still trapped in the ways of man. The Holy Spirit cannot be controlled by man and He is the one that works within the heart of man. The Holy Spirit brings about conviction of sin, releases people who are captive, and even prays for us.)

11. What does Simon's response show? (Acts 8:22-23 He responds with a cry for mercy from the Lord. His recognition of the truth of Peter's statement reveals the Spirit convicting him of his sin. God is forgiving, slow to anger, and rich in mercy. He is able to release Simon from captivity to sin.)

Application Questions:
1. What makes us great? (Acts 8:9-10 We can try to be great in the eyes of man, but that greatness will not last. To be great in the eyes of God is simply to believe the good news of the Lord Jesus. That is what brings you into the kingdom of God.)

2. How do we boast about ourselves or make ourselves great? (Acts 8:10 We try to control our own lives instead of looking to God. We worship material things more than the Lord. We seek pleasure over seeking Jesus.)

3. What visible things of man amaze us or capture our attention? (Acts 8:11 Our attention is easily drawn to new technology, amazed at creations of man, and quickly admire people that we view as great or talented.)

4. Where are the results of the kingdom of God visible to us today? (Acts 8:12 We can see the kingdom of God in creation, but even more specifically when someone believes in the Lord Jesus. The kingdom of God is visible in changed lives, in testimonies of faith, in sincere prayers, in baptism and at

communion where we receive forgiveness by the grace of God.)

5. Who should be baptized today? (Acts 8:12 Everyone; men, women, and children; who need the gift of the Holy Spirit. All who need to be washed clean from their sin, and everyone who is brought into the name of the Lord Jesus.)

6. How do we face the battle between the kingdom of God and the kingdom of man? (Acts 8:13 We can turn to the Lord in faith and then be distracted by the things of this world. Sometimes the battle is outward, but often it rages in the desires of our flesh. It is a battle that must daily be fought in the strength of the Lord.)

7. Who can strengthen us at weak times in our faith? (Acts 8:14-17 It is important to be a part of the church, the body of Christ, to help us stand when we are weak. The body of believers can pray for us and share the Word of God to help us stand when we are fragile.)

8. How do people view baptism today? (Acts 8:15 Some view it as a response of man to the faith that a person holds to. Others view it as a work of God where He is the one acting. In this text, they heard the Word of God, were baptized, and received the Holy Spirit.)

9. In what ways do we try to control the Holy Spirit like Simon? (Acts 8:18 Some try to create a spiritual atmosphere where people respond a certain way, such as healing, worship, or surrendering to God. Some will have people pray a certain prayer so that they get a certain result. Others guilt people into giving money in order to receive more blessings. There are many ways that we try to manipulate the Holy Spirit.)

10. Do we need the harsh rebuke that Peter gave to Simon? Where do we need to cry out for the Lord's mercy in our lives?

11. Does just entering a church or even professing Christ make you part of God's kingdom? (No, just entering a building does not change a person's heart; likewise, the tongue may be deceitful but it is God at work within you that make you part of His kingdom and His Church.)

15. Church Gathering
Acts 2:42-47 & Acts 18:1-11

Acts 2

[42]They devoted themselves to the apostles' teaching and to the fellowship, to the breaking of bread and to prayer. [43]Everyone was filled with awe, and many wonders and miraculous signs were done by the apostles. [44]All the believers were together and had everything in common. [45]Selling their possessions and goods, they gave to anyone as he had need. [46]Every day they continued to meet together in the temple courts. They broke bread in their homes and ate together with glad and sincere hearts, [47]praising God and enjoying the favor of all the people. And the Lord added to their number daily those who were being saved.

Acts 18

[1]After this, Paul left Athens and went to Corinth. [2]There he met a Jew named Aquila, a native of Pontus, who had recently come from Italy with his wife Priscilla, because Claudius had ordered all the Jews to leave Rome. Paul went to see them, [3]and because he was a tentmaker as they were, he stayed and worked with them. [4]Every Sabbath he reasoned in the synagogue, trying to persuade Jews and Greeks.

[5]When Silas and Timothy came from Macedonia, Paul devoted himself exclusively to preaching, testifying to the Jews that Jesus was the Christ. [6]But when the Jews opposed Paul and became abusive, he shook out his clothes in protest and said to them, "Your blood be on your own heads! I am clear of my responsibility. From now on I will go to the Gentiles."

[7]Then Paul left the synagogue and went next door to the house of Titius Justus, a worshiper of God. [8]Crispus, the synagogue ruler, and his entire household believed in the Lord; and many of the Corinthians who heard him believed and were baptized.

[9]One night the Lord spoke to Paul in a vision: "Do not be afraid; keep on speaking, do not be silent. [10]For I am with you, and no one is going to attack and harm you, because I have many people in this city." [11]So Paul stayed for a year and a half, teaching them the Word of God.

Study Questions: Church Gathering
Acts 2:42-47 & Acts 18:1-11

Introduction:
Acts chapter 2 describes the kind of church that everyone wants to be a part of. The people are growing in the Word of God, miracles are happening, people are sharing, everyone is glad and new believers are joining the church. Acts chapter 18 describes a different picture. The people in Corinth are abusive, the synagogue splits, a Christian church starts meeting next door and the synagogue leader joins that new church. Even Paul needed to be reminded to keep preaching and not to be afraid.

As members of a church, we are part of the body of Christ. While we are sinners, the one hope for the Church is that Christ is the head of the body. When we, as members of that body, submit to Him, then the whole body works together, but when we resist the Lord, then the body struggles. We must also be careful and not put our hope in salvation just because we go to church. Not all who are members of a church are believers. The primary role of the Church is to preach to the believer and the unbeliever. These two texts can encourage us and teach us how to care for the Church so that it looks like the bride of Christ that it was intended to be.

Grace Goals:

Knowledge
- To see the Church as our family and God as our Heavenly Father.
- To remember that the Church is Christ's body and He is the head. It is His kingdom on earth.

Attitude
- To delight in the fellowship in the local church and communion with believers around the world.

Actions
- To worship and share Jesus as a community of believers.
- To support the physical and spiritual needs of those in our fellowship as well as the larger body of Christ.
- To seek fellowship with other Christians centered on the Word of God.

Memory Verse:
Hebrews 10:25, "Let us not give up meeting together, as some are in the habit of doing, but let us encourage one another – and all the more as you see the Day approaching."

Questions about the Text:
1. How does the **Word of God** play a part in the early Church? (Acts 2:42; Acts 18:5, 11 In Acts 2, "They devoted themselves to the apostles' teaching." In Corinth, Paul dedicated himself exclusively to preaching and he stayed for a year and a half teaching them the Word of God.)

2. What role did **fellowship** have in the early Church? (Acts 2:42-46; 18:7, 8 They devoted themselves to fellowship. All the believers were together, had everything in common, and every day continued to meet in the temple courts. Even in Corinth, they met together weekly.)

3. Where does **worship** show up in the early Church? (Acts 2:42, 47; 18:7 They were breaking bread in remembrance of Jesus, praying, praising and are even described as worshipers of God.)

4. How do these texts show that **reaching out** was a part of who they were? (Acts 2:45, 47; 18:4, 8 They had an open attitude regarding anyone who had needs. Their concern for reaching out was also seen by the favor that they had with all of the people. In Corinth, Paul was trying to persuade the Jews and enlighten the Greeks. Many of the Corinthians believed and were baptized.)

5. How was **the Lord revealed** through these growing believers? (Acts 2:43, 47; 18:5, 8-10 The Lord was revealed through the "many wonders and miraculous signs" as well as the number of believers that were being added daily. In Corinth, Paul was preaching that Jesus was the Christ. Many who heard him believed and were baptized.)

6. How did the early Church get to the point where everyone was equal and that there were no needs among the believers? (Acts 2:45 The believers sold their possessions and goods in order to provide for fellow believers.)

7. What was the **attitude** of the members as they broke bread and ate together? (Acts 2:46 The believers came together and shared their food with glad and sincere hearts, praising God, and enjoying the favor of all people.)

8. How did the Church show that they were **meeting** real practical **needs**? (Acts 2:45; 18:3, 7 In Jerusalem, they gave to anyone as they had need. In Corinth, Paul stayed with Aquila and Priscilla and Titius Justus used his home as a meeting place for the new group.)

9. Why did the church in Corinth have struggles and a split? (Acts 18:6 The Jews, in Corinth, opposed Paul and became abusive to him. So, Paul shook out his clothes in protest and left. The people refused to believe in the Lord or to follow Him. Conflict comes from refusal to submit to the Lord and stubbornness to think that we are right.)

10. How does the Lord's message encourage Paul? (Acts 18:9 The Lord's message encouraged Paul, because He promised to be with him and protect him.)

Application Questions:

1. How does the **Word of God** change our lives? (Acts 2:42; Acts 18:5, 11 The Word of God changes us by teaching us about God, giving us a reason to worship. It changes us by showing us who we are and pointing us to the needs of people around us.)

2. How would someone describe the **fellowship** at our churches? (Acts 2:42-46; 18:7, 8 At times it might be full of "glad hearts" and at other times abusive because fellowship is made up of sinful people. Yet, when we submit to the Lord and His will, He makes our fellowship sweet. See 1 John 3:11-20)

3. How can **worship** be a simple and beautiful response to the Lord rather than an entertainment show? (Acts 2:42, 47; 18:7 The early church had a very simple form of worship. It focused on teaching the Word of God, remembering Jesus sacrifice, baptisms, prayer and praising God.)

4. How can we **reach** the world around us? (Acts 2:45, 47; 18:4, 8 We can be reaching out by meeting people's

needs and sharing what Jesus has done in our lives.)

5. What would a welcoming open **attitude** look like in our
    churches? (Acts 2:44-47 Acts 2 describes good fellowship,
    teaching and worship. It describes people who are filled with
    awe. They are united and they are sharing. An open attitude is
    one where the people are glad, sincere and people are joining
    them. John 13:34-35)

6. How can people see **the Lord revealed** in our churches? (Acts
    2:43, 47; 18:5, 8-10 Through the faithful preaching of God's
    Word and sincere worship, resulting in people being saved.)

7. What happens when the Word of God is no longer the center
    of the fellowship we share as the Church? (We fail to fulfill
    the Great Commission and we fail to sharpen each other and
    strengthen each other in faith. We merely come together for
    the sake of something to do but our purpose is selfish and
    empty.)

8. How can we show love to those who are directly involved in
    our local church? The church abroad? (Romans 12:6-8; 1 John
    4:7-21)

9. Why is attending a church needed for the believer? (It is
    essential for the life of a believer to receive the fellowship,
    encouragement, and accountability from being together as a
    body. Hebrews 10:23-25 says, "Do not give up meeting
    together.")

10. How can you assist your local church body? (Being a part of
    the body, using your gifts, Romans 12:4-8 and 1 Corinthians
    12.)

11. What should be some of the natural results of the body of
    Christ coming together for fellowship around the Word of
    God? (Acts 2:46-47 Glad and sincere hearts, a desire to praise
    and worship God, and the respect of all the people.)

12. How can the Lord direct our churches and empower us to go
    forward in ministry? (Acts 2:47; Acts 18:10 We should keep
    Him in the center of everything we do through His Word and
    His Spirit. We need His guidance and protection.)

13. How can you help and support those who are involved in the ministry?

14. Why is ministry and caring for the church difficult? (Acts 18:6 Caring for the church can be a struggle because there are those who directly oppose ministry, even to the point of abuse. Satan will also try to ruin attempts to promote God's will in the congregation. We must realize that all of those who are within the church are still daily struggling with their sinful flesh and not demand someone to be perfect as we ourselves are unable to be perfect.)

15. Do you need encouragement from the Lord regarding your ministry? (Acts 18:9-10 Like the Lord told Paul, "Do not be afraid; keep on speaking, do not be silent. For I am with you.")

16. Church Orderliness
1 Corinthians 14:26-40

1 Corinthians 14

26 What then shall we say, brothers? When you come together, everyone has a hymn, or a word of instruction, a revelation, a tongue or an interpretation. All of these must be done for the strengthening of the church.

27 If anyone speaks in a tongue, two-- or at the most three-- should speak, one at a time, and someone must interpret. 28 If there is no interpreter, the speaker should keep quiet in the church and speak to himself and God. 29 Two or three prophets should speak, and the others should weigh carefully what is said.

30 And if a revelation comes to someone who is sitting down, the first speaker should stop. 31 For you can all prophesy in turn so that everyone may be instructed and encouraged. 32 The spirits of prophets are subject to the control of prophets.

33 For God is not a God of disorder but of peace. As in all the congregations of the saints, 34 women should remain silent in the churches. They are not allowed to speak, but must be in submission, as the Law says. 35 If they want to inquire about something, they should ask their own husbands at home; for it is disgraceful for a woman to speak in the church.

36 Did the word of God originate with you? Or are you the only people it has reached? 37 If anybody thinks he is a prophet or spiritually gifted, let him acknowledge that what I am writing to you is the Lord's command. 38 If he ignores this, he himself will be ignored.

39 Therefore, my brothers, be eager to prophesy, and do not forbid speaking in tongues.

40 But everything should be done in a fitting and orderly way.

Study Questions: Church Orderliness
1 Corinthians 14:26-40

Introduction:
Whenever people meet, leadership, schedule, and order need to be addressed. In the church, people will have different ideas of how to lead, styles of music, types of prayer, and who should preach. Some things are not defined in the Bible, but we are clearly told other things. The believers must decide how things will be handled in their own church, but this lesson describes some important guidelines that the Lord gave to the church in Corinth.

Grace Goals:
Knowledge
- To know the importance of clarity and order in worship for the strengthening of the church.
- To understand God's clear instructions for clarity and order.

Attitude
- To be self-controlled in what to say or how to say it.
- To respect the Lord's instructions even if they are difficult.

Actions
- To maintain an orderly worship service.
- To listen carefully to what is said from the Lord.

Questions about the Text:
1. What is the purpose of meeting together as a church?
   (1 Corinthians 14:26 This verse says that "all of these things must be done for the strengthening of the church." Discussions about style, order, or leadership must begin by discussing how these can be used to strengthen the church.)

2. What did worship look like for the church of Corinth?
   (1 Corinthians 14:26 Coming together, music, instructions, revelation, a tongue, or an interpretation.)

3. How did the Lord instruct them through Paul regarding their use of tongues? (1 Corinthians 14:27-8 It should be limited to two or at the most three people with each one taking turns. If there is no interpreter the speaker should keep quiet in the church and speak to himself and God. Speaking in a language that others do not understand does not strengthen the church.)

4. What was their instruction regarding the prophet or the one telling the Word of God? (1 Corinthians 14:29 It should be limited to two or three while the others listen carefully to what they say. The one speaking on behalf of the Lord carries an important role in clearly communicating God's Word.)

5. What did they need to hear regarding someone with a revelation? (1 Corinthians 14:30-32 They should not speak unless the one speaking stops. The purpose is restated "so that everyone may be instructed and encouraged.")

6. Why were all of these instructions given to them? (1 Corinthians 14:33 The statement "For God is not a God of disorder but of peace" describes the problem that they were having. The people were excited about their faith and understanding so they were quick to speak but slow to listen. The statements regarding strengthening the church, weighing carefully what is said, being instructed, and encouraged are the main points they needed to hear.)

7. How are we to understand the verses about women speaking? (1 Corinthians 14:33-35 The important context of these verses is regarding tongues, prophets, and a revelation from the Lord. It refers to women being in submission or under authority. It is tempting to modify these statements by adding our own thoughts rather than leaving them as they are. Paul says, "what I am writing to you is the Lord's command.")

8. Why did Paul include verses 36-38? (1 Corinthians 14:36-38 The instructions that Paul is passing on to the Corinthians is hard to accept. He points out that this is the Word of God, that they are not the only ones to receive this message, and even that this is the practice in all the congregations in verse 33.)

9. What is Paul's summarizing thought? (1 Corinthians 14:39-40 The purpose of these instructions is to ensure order and the building up of the believers. That is done primarily through prophecy or communicating the Word of God, but can also be done through the speaking of tongues.)

Application Questions:
1. Why do we meet together as a church? (1 Corinthians 14:26 We also meet together to be strengthened in our faith. Style, order, and leadership can be either helpful or distracting.)

2. How does your church compare to Corinth? What parts strengthen your faith or what parts distract from it?

3. What would the Lord instruct us regarding the use of tongues? (1 Corinthians 14:27-8 Speaking a language that others do not understand does not strengthen our churches. Yet, the Lord does speak to people and through people with the gift of tongues and if spoken in a worship service, it should be accompanied with translation.)

4. What priority should the Word of God have in our worship? (1 Corinthians 14:29 It should be a high priority. The one speaking should carefully prepare what is said and the listeners should weigh carefully what is said.)

5. What does a revelation from God look like? (1 Corinthians 14:30-32 The two clear revelations from God are His written word, scriptures, and His living Word, Jesus. Any information or word from the Lord needs to be in accordance with these two clear revelations.)

6. What things cause disorder in our worship times and what things strengthen the church? (1 Corinthians 14:33 A manipulation of the people through emotion, guilt, or fear can cause disorder and unrest. The Word of God is that which strengthens the church.)

7. What role should women have in the church? (1 Corinthians 14:33-35 The Bible is full of ministry roles for women in the church. Bible scholars disagree on these verses, but the plain reading of the text would not have women teaching over men. See Titus 2:3-5.)

8. When we disagree with God's teaching on some specific point, what should our response be? (1 Corinthians 14:36-38 God's Word must become the authority over our feelings and wishes. If there is a difficult passage of scripture, we need to submit our will to the word.)

9. Where might we need to make changes in our worship so that everything is done in a fitting and orderly way and so that the believers are being built up?

17. Church Revealed
Revelation 2:1-17

1 "To the angel of the church in **Ephesus** write: These are the words of him who holds the seven stars in his right hand and walks among the seven golden lampstands:
2 I know your deeds, your hard work and your perseverance. I know that you cannot tolerate wicked men, that you have tested those who claim to be apostles but are not, and have found them false.
3 You have persevered and have endured hardships for my name, and have not grown weary.
4 Yet I hold this against you: You have forsaken your first love.
5 Remember the height from which you have fallen! Repent and do the things you did at first. If you do not repent, I will come to you and remove your lampstand from its place.
6 But you have this in your favor: You hate the practices of the Nicolaitans, which I also hate.
7 He who has an ear, let him hear what the Spirit says to the churches. To him who overcomes, I will give the right to eat from the tree of life, which is in the paradise of God.

8 "To the angel of the church in **Smyrna** write: These are the words of him who is the First and the Last, who died and came to life again.
9 I know your afflictions and your poverty-- yet you are rich! I know the slander of those who say they are Jews and are not, but are a synagogue of Satan.
10 Do not be afraid of what you are about to suffer. I tell you, the devil will put some of you in prison to test you, and you will suffer persecution for ten days. Be faithful, even to the point of death, and I will give you the crown of life.
11 He who has an ear, let him hear what the Spirit says to the churches. He who overcomes will not be hurt at all by the second death.

12 "To the angel of the church in **Pergamum** write: These are the words of him who has the sharp, double-edged sword.
13 I know where you live-- where Satan has his throne. Yet you remain true to my name. You did not renounce your faith in me, even in the days of Antipas, my faithful witness, who was put to death in your city-- where Satan lives.
14 Nevertheless, I have a few things against you: You have people there who hold to the teaching of Balaam, who taught Balak to entice the Israelites to sin by eating food sacrificed to idols and by committing sexual immorality.

15 Likewise you also have those who hold to the teaching of the Nicolaitans.

16 Repent therefore! Otherwise, I will soon come to you and will fight against them with the sword of my mouth.

17 He who has an ear, let him hear what the Spirit says to the churches. To him who overcomes, I will give some of the hidden manna. I will also give him a white stone with a new name written on it, known only to him who receives it.

Study Questions: Church Revealed
Revelation 2:1-17

Introduction:
Revelation 2:1-3:22 is written to seven different churches. Each church has unique things for which they are encouraged and other areas that in which they are corrected. Notice each church begins with the statement, "These are the words" referring to Jesus' words. For each church, Jesus is described in different ways, but it is Jesus who is referred to each time. Notice also the statement, "I know your deeds." That statement reveals the churches hidden sin as well as their faithfulness and perseverance. In the same way God's Word both warns us and encourages us. Each of the statements to the churches ends with "let him hear what the Spirit says to the churches." That challenge is for the churches and each individual who studies this lesson. May the Word of God and the Spirit of God give direction to the church, rather than the authority of man.

Grace Goals:
Knowledge
– To understand that Jesus knows His churches personally.
– To learn the common problems that churches can face.

Attitude
– To humbly receive the words of correction.
– To be encouraged by the heart of Jesus for His churches.

Actions
– To repent and return to a personal walk with Christ.
– To stand firm in the faith through all trials.

Questions about the Text:
1. Who is the one speaking to the churches? Why is that important? (Jesus is described in each of the seven churches with a different description each time. It is important because He is the head of the church and these are His words to His people.)

2. What do the words "These are the words" and "I will" say to the churches? (Jesus encourages them with this His personal letter. "I will" – is a promise and a confident statement of what is going to happen. Jesus knows His church, He has authority over them, and they are a part of His kingdom.)

3.   What do the words, "I know your deeds mean for the churches? ("I know your deeds." – He knows their hard work, trials, love, and perseverance. They are not alone although they may feel lonely. He also knows their failures, their sin, and their cold hearts.)

4.   Why does Jesus say, "Let him hear what the Spirit says to the churches"? (He is saying, take encouragement and be warned with the words that apply to you. This is an opportunity for some of the churches to repent and for others to persevere.)

5.   **Ephesus** – What is their encouragement and their warning? (Revelation 2:1-7 They have worked hard, persevered, identified wicked men, tested false prophets, endured hardships, and not grown weary, but they have left their first love. It is possible to do all the right actions without the right motives.)

6.   **Smyrna** – What is their encouragement? (Revelation 2:8-11 Life has been difficult for them. They have faced afflictions, poverty, slander, now soon prison, persecution, and death. The trials they face on this earth will be over soon and their future gain will be incomparable to the things that they have had to endure.)

7.   **Pergamum** – What is their encouragement and their warning? (Revelation 2:12-17 They have remained true to Jesus and did not renounce their faith even though they live where Satan has his throne. In spite of their faithfulness, they have immorality in their church and have allowed those with false teaching in their midst.)

Application Questions:

1.   How does Jesus speak to us today? (He has given us His Word and even these specific letters to the churches.)

2.   What encouragement or promises does Jesus have for us? (He loves us, knows what we are going through, and is still in charge.)

3.   What does Jesus know about us? (He knows all that we do both good and bad. That is both a comfort and a fearful thing.)

4. The Lord gives us a personal letter in His word. How do we respond to what Jesus says to us? (It can be easy to take the Word of God for granted rather than as a personal message. We also need to "hear what the Spirit says.")

5. **Ephesus** – When have we done the right actions but with the wrong motives? (Revelation 2:1-7 The list could be long, but it begins when we are doing things for God out of obligation rather than because of our love for Him.)

6. **Smyrna** – When has life been difficult for us even to the point of death? (Revelation 2:8-11 Life can be difficult and persecution can be crushing, but the promise of eternal life changes everything for the believer. In those times, we need to remember that He knows our afflictions and that He will give us the crown of life.)

7. **Pergamum** – When have we allowed false teaching into our lives even teaching that leads to sin? (Revelation 2:12-17 False teaching creeps into our thoughts when we entertain ideas that are against God's word. In the garden, Satan asked Eve, "Did God really say?" which led to their sin.)

18. Church Revealed
Revelation 2:18-3:22

2:18 "To the angel of the church in **Thyatira** write: These are the words of the Son of God, whose eyes are like blazing fire and whose feet are like burnished bronze.

19 I know your deeds, your love and faith, your service and perseverance, and that you are now doing more than you did at first.

20 Nevertheless, I have this against you: You tolerate that woman Jezebel, who calls herself a prophetess. By her teaching she misleads my servants into sexual immorality and the eating of food sacrificed to idols.

21 I have given her time to repent of her immorality, but she is unwilling.

22 So I will cast her on a bed of suffering, and I will make those who commit adultery with her suffer intensely, unless they repent of her ways.

23 I will strike her children dead. Then all the churches will know that I am he who searches hearts and minds, and I will repay each of you according to your deeds.

24 Now I say to the rest of you in Thyatira, to you who do not hold to her teaching and have not learned Satan's so-called deep secrets (I will not impose any other burden on you):

25 Only hold on to what you have until I come.

26 To him who overcomes and does my will to the end, I will give authority over the nations--

27 'He will rule them with an iron scepter; he will dash them to pieces like pottery'--just as I have received authority from my Father.

28 I will also give him the morning star.

29 He who has an ear, let him hear what the Spirit says to the churches.

3:1 "To the angel of the church in **Sardis** write: These are the words of him who holds the seven spirits of God and the seven stars. I know your deeds; you have a reputation of being alive, but you are dead.

2 Wake up! Strengthen what remains and is about to die, for I have not found your deeds complete in the sight of my God.

3 Remember, therefore, what you have received and heard; obey it, and repent. But if you do not wake up, I will come like a thief, and you will not know at what time I will come to you.

4 Yet you have a few people in Sardis who have not soiled their clothes. They will walk with me, dressed in white, for they are worthy.

5 He who overcomes will, like them, be dressed in white. I will never blot out his name from the book of life, but will acknowledge his name before my Father and his angels.
6 He who has an ear, let him hear what the Spirit says to the churches.

7 "To the angel of the church in **Philadelphia** write: These are the words of him who is holy and true, who holds the key of David. What he opens no one can shut, and what he shuts no one can open.
8 I know your deeds. See, I have placed before you an open door that no one can shut. I know that you have little strength, yet you have kept my word and have not denied my name.
9 I will make those who are of the synagogue of Satan, who claim to be Jews though they are not, but are liars-- I will make them come and fall down at your feet and acknowledge that I have loved you.
10 Since you have kept my command to endure patiently, I will also keep you from the hour of trial that is going to come upon the whole world to test those who live on the earth.
11 I am coming soon. Hold on to what you have, so that no one will take your crown.
12 Him who overcomes I will make a pillar in the temple of my God. Never again will he leave it. I will write on him the name of my God and the name of the city of my God, the new Jerusalem, which is coming down out of heaven from my God; and I will also write on him my new name.
13 He who has an ear, let him hear what the Spirit says to the churches.

14 "To the angel of the church in **Laodicea** write: These are the words of the Amen, the faithful and true witness, the ruler of God's creation.
15 I know your deeds, that you are neither cold nor hot. I wish you were either one or the other!
16 So, because you are lukewarm-- neither hot nor cold-- I am about to spit you out of my mouth.
17 You say, 'I am rich; I have acquired wealth and do not need a thing.' But you do not realize that you are wretched, pitiful, poor, blind and naked.
18 I counsel you to buy from me gold refined in the fire, so you can become rich; and white clothes to wear, so you can cover your shameful nakedness; and salve to put on your eyes, so you can see.
19 Those whom I love I rebuke and discipline. So be earnest, and repent.
20 Here I am! I stand at the door and knock. If anyone hears my voice and opens the door, I will come in and eat with him, and he with me.

21 To him who overcomes, I will give the right to sit with me on my throne, just as I overcame and sat down with my Father on his throne. 22 He who has an ear, let him hear what the Spirit says to the churches."

Study Questions: Church Revealed
Revelation 2:18-3:22

Questions about the Text:

1. **Thyatira** – What is their encouragement and their warning?
    (Revelation 2:18-29 They also have been faithful in their love,
    service, perseverance, and their efforts to do more. Some have
    followed after immorality and idol worship but others have
    been faithful to following Christ alone. The warnings for the
    first are harsh and the encouragement for the second is dear.)

2. **Sardis** – What is their encouragement and warnings?
    (Revelation 3:1-6 A few have remained faithful and will walk
    with Jesus in glory. However, most of them have a dead faith,
    they are not living out what they had received and heard. They
    will lose what they have been given unless they turn and
    repent.)

3. **Philadelphia** – What is their encouragement? (Revelation 3:7-
    13 They have been weak faithful. They have kept the Word of
    God, they have not denied Jesus, and they have endured
    patiently. Jesus promises to keep them from the trial coming
    upon the whole world.)

4. **Laodicea** – What is their warning? (Revelation 3:14-22 They
    have failed to keep their passion for Jesus. Their material
    possessions have hidden the fact that they are wretched,
    pitiful, poor, blind, and naked. The grace of God gives them
    this rebuke and this warning. The Lord patiently stands at the
    door knocking, calling, waiting, and longing to come in to
    them.)

Application Questions:

1. **Thyatira** – How can one protected sin corrupt the many good
    things that we do? (Revelation 2:18-29 Sin has its origin in a
    man's heart. One protected sin will corrupt the heart and all of
    the good that comes out from it.)

2. **Sardis** – When could we have a reputation of a living faith
    when our faith is nearly dead? (Revelation 3:1-6 This is
    especially dangerous for church leaders facing burnout
    because it is possible to put on a mask before others and yet
    inside they are dying.)

3. **Philadelphia** When is our strength gone to the point that we can barely hold on? – (Revelation 3:7-13 There are many things that cause us to be physically weary and other things that can drain us emotionally. For those in Philadelphia, they were beaten down because of their faith.)

4. **Laodicea** – When do we just go through the motions of life and faith? (Revelation 3:14-22 When things are physically easy for us we can become lazy in our faith. We can trust in ourselves rather than depend on the Lord. The Lord will discipline those that He loves and He will knock on the door of our heart, waiting to be invited in.)

5. Whose authority is your church ultimately under?

19. Church Gifting
1 Corinthians 12:12-31

12 The body is a unit, though it is made up of many parts; and though all its parts are many, they form one body. So it is with Christ.

13 For we were all baptized by one Spirit into one body-- whether Jews or Greeks, slave or free-- and we were all given the one Spirit to drink.

14 Now the body is not made up of one part but of many.

15 If the foot should say, "Because I am not a hand, I do not belong to the body," it would not for that reason cease to be part of the body.

16 And if the ear should say, "Because I am not an eye, I do not belong to the body," it would not for that reason cease to be part of the body.

17 If the whole body were an eye, where would the sense of hearing be? If the whole body were an ear, where would the sense of smell be?

18 But in fact God has arranged the parts in the body, every one of them, just as he wanted them to be.

19 If they were all one part, where would the body be?

20 As it is, there are many parts, but one body.

21 The eye cannot say to the hand, "I don't need you!" And the head cannot say to the feet, "I don't need you!"

22 On the contrary, those parts of the body that seem to be weaker are indispensable,

23 and the parts that we think are less honorable we treat with special honor. And the parts that are unpresentable are treated with special modesty,

24 while our presentable parts need no special treatment. But God has combined the members of the body and has given greater honor to the parts that lacked it,

25 so that there should be no division in the body, but that its parts should have equal concern for each other.

26 If one part suffers, every part suffers with it; if one part is honored, every part rejoices with it.

27 Now you are the body of Christ, and each one of you is a part of it.

28 And in the church God has appointed first of all apostles, second prophets, third teachers, then workers of miracles, also those having gifts of healing, those able to help others, those with gifts of administration, and those speaking in different kinds of tongues.

29 Are all apostles? Are all prophets? Are all teachers? Do all work miracles?

30 Do all have gifts of healing? Do all speak in tongues? Do all interpret?

31 But eagerly desire the greater gifts. And now I will show you the most excellent way.

Study Questions: Church Gifting
1 Corinthians 12:12-31

Introduction:

Churches must work together to serve God's kingdom in order that the body of Christ can be built up. The Lord has given the members of the local church different gifts. When the people work together using their gifts, the church will function as the body of Christ. The example of the church as a body is helpful to understand practically how the believers are intended to work together. A healthy body is strong and can do amazing things but a sick or injured body can struggle to just survive. The church and the members of that church body are the first introduction people have to Jesus. That is an opportunity and a responsibility.

Grace Goals:

Knowledge
– To understand how the body of Christ is to function together.
– To realize that every part of the church is needed.

Attitude
– To respect the other parts of the church without looking down on ourselves or each other.
– To avoid division and have equal concern for each other.

Actions
– To fulfill the responsibilities of the gifts we have been given.
– To eagerly seek the greater gifts.

Questions about the Text:

1. What is the purpose of the body? (1 Corinthians 12:12 The body is intended to be one unit. It is be connected together, functioning together, and one in function with each part working toward a common goal.)

2. How does the church work like a body? (1 Corinthians 12:13 There is one baptism and one Spirit. Regardless of cultural background or economic position the one Spirit gives life to everyone in the same way. It is that Spirit of God that connects people from diverse backgrounds into Christ's body.)

3. What causes the parts of the body to feel disconnected? (1 Corinthians 12:14-16, 21 One way is for one part of the body to see itself as insignificant or less important compared

to another part of the body. One can see another function as more important or can see its own role as insignificant.

Also a part of the body could think or say that it doesn't need some part of the body. Perhaps it sees its own role as the most important or cannot see the value of the other part.)

4. Why are all of the parts of the body needed? (1 Corinthians 12:17 Each part of the body provides a unique and vital role. Without the individual members the body is not able to function as it was designed.)

5. Why did God arrange the parts of the body as He did? (1 Corinthians 12:18 He created the parts to be dependent on each other. Each part has a unique function and the body can not function without all of the parts.)

6. How can the parts of the body be viewed as unique or special? (1 Corinthians 12:22-24 He has created some parts to be weaker, others to have less honor, and some parts to be private. Yet those same parts are essential, honorable, and special. God created each part with its own role.)

7. What is the goal of the body? (1 Corinthians 12:24-26 The body must function together as members of one whole. There should be no division but in fact the parts of the body need to have concern for each other. Verse 26 says it very clearly, "If one part suffers, every part suffers with it; if one part is honored, every part rejoices with it.")

8. How do these various parts of the body of Christ serve the church? (1 Corinthians 12:27-28
- Apostles were those 12 men that were specifically called by Jesus. The term apostle means sent out ones.
- Prophets are those that tell forth the Word of God. Their role is to apply God's Word to our lives. They are the preachers.
- Teachers are those that explain the Word of God. They can clarify difficult passages and connect scripture to scripture.
- Miracle workers are those that the Lord uses to show His greatness. It is God's power that enables them to do great things and these things point to the Savior.
- Healers are used to bring God's healing to the bodies of those who are sick. Healing can come immediately or through care and medicine.

- Helpers are able to see the needs of others and come alongside of them. It is a gift to recognize the needs of others.
- Administration are those that care for the details of the functions of the body including organization and finances.
- Tongues is also one of the gifts that allows a person to communicate a message of God in an unknown language (used together with the gift of interpretation of tongues – 1 Cor. 12:10.) It is also used individually as special prayer focus with the Lord.
See also Ephesians 4:11-16)

9. How do these various gifts need each other? (1 Corinthians 12:29-31 The apostles themselves sought others to help them such as Stephen. Each of them needs the others because without all of the gifts there are areas of ministry that are missed.)

10. What is the most excellent way? (1 Corinthians 12:29-31 Love is the most excellent way and the whole next chapter describes it. Love makes it possible for these various parts of the body to work together. Without love these acts are worthless.)

Application Questions:
1. How do our bodies function? (1 Corinthians 12:12 Our bodies work together as our head directs it. The parts work together smoothly without notice until one part is injured.)

2. Do our churches work like a body? (1 Corinthians 12:13 Our churches are also united by one baptism and one Spirit, but often times we judge or criticize others without seeing our need of them.)

3. What causes our bodies to function poorly? (1 Corinthians 12:14-16, 21 When a part of our body gets injured the effects can be felt throughout the entire body. When we stop using a part of our body, such as our feet or hands, the rest of the body is affected as well.)

4. Are there any parts of our church that we don't need? (1 Corinthians 12:17 No, we need every part. Some of the functions get less notice, but are still needed to make the whole work.)

5. Did God give some people all of the abilities for the church? (1 Corinthians 12:18 No, He made us dependent on one another. Some have more visible gifts, but all of the gifts are needed.)

6. What parts of the church have special and often unnoticed value? (1 Corinthians 12:22-24 The people that clean the building, the ones that organize the food, and the people who welcome visitors can go unnoticed but are vitally important.)

7. What is the goal of the church? (1 Corinthians 12:24-26 The goal of the church is to serve the head, Jesus. To do that, the church needs to work together rather than arguing or complaining about other people.)

8. What are the parts that make up a well-functioning church? (1 Corinthians 12:27-28 The pastor has a primary role as He cares for the people and preaches the Word of God. Other leaders are also important: musicians, those watching the children, singers, those who give, those who care for the sick, teachers, etc. The list can be long.)

9. Do the people in your church see their need of each other?

10. How is love expressed in your congregation?

20. Church Unity
1 Corinthians 3:1-11 & Acts 15:1-12

1 Corinthians 3

[1]Brothers, I could not address you as spiritual but as worldly—mere infants in Christ. [2]I gave you milk, not solid food, for you were not yet ready for it. Indeed, you are still not ready. [3]You are still worldly. For since there is jealousy and quarreling among you, are you not worldly? Are you not acting like mere men? [4]For when one says, "I follow Paul," and another, "I follow Apollos," are you not mere men?

[5]What, after all, is Apollos? And what is Paul? Only servants, through whom you came to believe—as the Lord has assigned to each his task. [6]I planted the seed, Apollos watered it, but God made it grow. [7]So neither he who plants nor he who waters is anything, but only God, who makes things grow. [8]The man who plants and the man who waters have one purpose, and each will be rewarded according to his own labor. [9]For we are God's fellow workers; you are God's field, God's building.

[10]By the grace God has given me, I laid a foundation as an expert builder, and someone else is building on it. But each one should be careful how he builds. [11]For no one can lay any foundation other than the one already laid, which is Jesus Christ.

Acts 15

[1]Some men came down from Judea to Antioch and were teaching the brothers: "Unless you are circumcised, according to the custom taught by Moses, you cannot be saved." [2]This brought Paul and Barnabas into sharp dispute and debate with them. So Paul and Barnabas were appointed, along with some other believers, to go up to Jerusalem to see the apostles and elders about this question. [3]The church sent them on their way, and as they traveled through Phoenicia and Samaria, they told how the Gentiles had been converted. This news made all the brothers very glad. [4]When they came to Jerusalem, they were welcomed by the church and the apostles and elders, to whom they reported everything God had done through them.
[5]Then some of the believers who belonged to the party of the Pharisees stood up and said, "The Gentiles must be circumcised and required to obey the Law of Moses."

[6]The apostles and elders met to consider this question. [7]After much discussion, Peter got up and addressed them: "Brothers, you know that some time ago God made a choice among you that the Gentiles might hear from my lips the message of the gospel and believe. [8]God, who knows the heart, showed that he accepted them by giving the Holy

Spirit to them, just as he did to us. [9]He made no distinction between us and them, for he purified their hearts by faith. [10]Now then, why do you try to test God by putting on the necks of the disciples a yoke that neither we nor our fathers have been able to bear? [11]No! We believe it is through the grace of our Lord Jesus that we are saved, just as they are."

[12]The whole assembly became silent as they listened to Barnabas and Paul telling about the miraculous signs and wonders God had done among the Gentiles through them.

Study Questions: Church Unity
1 Corinthians 3:1-11 & Acts 15:1-12

Introduction:
The church in Corinth struggled with many of the same things that we struggle with in our churches today. There were various opinions about Apollos' leadership versus Paul's authority and there was jealousy and quarreling because the church had lost their foundation on Jesus. The same type of struggle showed up in Antioch over circumcision. When they brought the matter to the church in Jerusalem the topic had the potential of splitting the early church. After the apostles and elders discussed the issue, they found the solution was to bring it right back to Jesus and His grace.

Like a family, the church family can also have problems because its members are sinners. It is essential that we bring problems back to the one foundation, Jesus, and work through the problems. Church unity is not the absence of problems, but the decision to work through the problems. We must not run from the conflicts, but rather look to Jesus for a way to solve them. Romans 15:5 says, "May the God who gives endurance and encouragement give you a spirit of unity among yourselves as you follow Christ Jesus."

Grace Goals:
   Knowledge
   –   To understand that if Christ is the head of the body, then there is only one body.
   –   To realize that we are servants of the Lord and our only purpose is to bring Him glory.

   Attitude
   –   To appreciate the differences that God has made in each member of His body.

   Actions
   –   To listen and understand other people's perspectives.
   –   To encourage fellow brothers and sisters in the body of Christ.
   –   To unite as a body reaching the world for Christ.

Memory Verse:
1 Peter 3:8 "Finally, all of you, live in harmony with one another; be sympathetic, love as brothers, be compassionate and humble."

Questions about the Story:

1. How does Paul view the Corinthian church? (1 Corinthians 3:1-4 He told them that he viewed them as infants in Christ, worldly, jealous, quarrelsome and mere men.)

2. How are Paul and Apollos' character described? (1 Corinthians 3:5-9 They have a servant attitude and are working at their assigned task. They recognize that the work they do is nothing because only God can make it grow. They are working for one purpose, the Lord's glory.)

3. What is the problem with focusing on two different leaders? (1 Corinthians 3:3-4 Following two leaders will always lead down two separate paths. If we are following Jesus, then there is only one leader and one foundation.)

4. How does a leader help the church? (1 Corinthians 3:5-9 They must serve the church, plant the seeds of faith in people, water that faith with the Word of God and watch the Lord grow people for use in His kingdom.)

5. How do leaders hurt the church? (1 Corinthians 3:3-4 They allow jealousy, quarreling and immature attitudes to develop. Any amount of personal pride destroys the focus on what the Lord has done.)

6. What is the leader's role verses God's? (1 Corinthians 3:5-11 The leader can only do the task they have been assigned. Even that work is the grace of God. The Lord is the one that causes people to believe and He is the one that makes them grow. The very foundation is Jesus alone.)

7. How does the Lord receive glory? (1 Corinthians 3:9-11 When the church works together, people are saved, the Word of God is taught and the living temple of God is constructed.)

8. Why does Paul give a caution about how to build on the foundation of Christ? (1 Corinthians 3:10 Because there is no other foundation other than Jesus Christ.)

9. Why was the topic of circumcision so important? (Acts 15:1 It was a matter of salvation. It was a physical sign of membership in the Jewish community. It was a huge cultural jump for the Jews to accept that Gentiles could be saved. It

was even a greater jump to set aside the circumcision that God had established with Abraham.)

10. How was the teaching that the men brought from Judea to Antioch harmful? (Acts 15:1 It brought doubt about how people are saved. It caused questions and doubt about the two founding teachers in Antioch. It forced the issue to be brought to Jerusalem.)

11. How did the church in Antioch respond to the debate that came up in their church? (Acts 15:2-3 The church appointed Paul and Barnabas, along with some other believers, to go up to Jerusalem to see the apostles and elders about this question about circumcision for Gentile believers.)

12. How does Paul and Barnabas' testimony encourage church unity? (Acts 15:3-4 Paul and Barnabas reported all that God had done and how the Gentiles had been converted. It was a focus on the Lord's work that brought about unity.)

13. How did the apostles and elders respond to believers who belonged to the Pharisees? (Acts 15:6-11 They met to consider and discuss the question. Then Peter explained that God had accepted the Gentiles by giving them the Holy Spirit and had made no distinction between them and the Jews. Peter pointed out that it is only through the grace of the Lord Jesus that there is salvation.)

Application Questions:
1. What appearance does the church give to the outside world when we fight, quarrel, and argue? (1 Corinthians 3:1-4 The world thinks of it as the same as itself, if not worse because of the hypocritical lifestyle of promoting love and peace but living in anger and dissension. This is what Christ was talking about in John 13:35, "By this all men will know that you are my disciples, if you love one another." 1 Corinthians 6:5-8)

2. How should we respond when arguments and debates come up in church? (1 Corinthians 3:5; Acts 15:2, 8, 11 We should take the attitude of servants and humble ourselves before God. Then we should take the issue to leadership and seek the Lord. Finally, the decision must come as the whole church is united in God's Word. Ephesians 4:1-3; 1 Peter 3:8-11)

3. What is the problem when we follow the leadership of man rather than Jesus? (1 Corinthians 3:3-4 We begin to compare ourselves with others. In the process envy, jealousy, and quarrels develop.)

4. How should we view our position in the ministry of God? (1 Corinthians 3:5-6 We should view ourselves as mere servants of the Lord Jesus Christ, appointed to do that which He would have us to do.)

5. What are some ways that you can be serving your church body? (Romans 12:3-8)

6. How do we help or hurt the church? (1 Corinthians 3:3-9 We help the church when we focus on Jesus and help people grow. We hurt the church anytime our pride gets involved. Every fruit produced comes not because we create it, but the Lord has. Psalm 133)

7. How can we stay united in ministry? (Acts 15:3-4, 11-12 We must focus on our salvation through Jesus and the work that the Lord is doing. Hebrews 10:23-25; 1 John 3:11-20)

8. What are some ways that you have seen the Lord actively working in your congregation?

9. Why does all of the honor and praise need to go to the Lord if anything good comes out of our ministry? (1 Corinthians 3:7 God alone must receive the glory because He causes fruit and growth in the ministry.)

10. What are we to do in the church when we don't know or understand what our ministry is? (1 Corinthians 3:5-8 We should seek God, as He ultimately is the one who appoints and determines the work that we are to be about and is the one who works through us. Other Christians may assist us in seeing how God has blessed us or is leading us.)

11. What foundation should our ministries be built on? (1 Corinthians 3:10-11; Acts 15:11 Our lives and ministries must be built on the foundation of Christ. It is only through the grace of God that are we saved. He is a solid rock while any other foundation is sinking sand. 1 John 4:7-21)

21. Church Cooperation
Romans 1:8-14 & Colossians 1:3-9

Romans 1

8 First, I thank my God through Jesus Christ for all of you, because your faith is being reported all over the world.

9 God, whom I serve with my whole heart in preaching the gospel of his Son, is my witness how constantly I remember you

10 in my prayers at all times; and I pray that now at last by God's will the way may be opened for me to come to you.

11 I long to see you so that I may impart to you some spiritual gift to make you strong--

12 that is, that you and I may be mutually encouraged by each other's faith.

13 I do not want you to be unaware, brothers, that I planned many times to come to you (but have been prevented from doing so until now) in order that I might have a harvest among you, just as I have had among the other Gentiles.

14 I am obligated both to Greeks and non-Greeks, both to the wise and the foolish.

15 That is why I am so eager to preach the gospel also to you who are at Rome.

16 I am not ashamed of the gospel, because it is the power of God for the salvation of everyone who believes: first for the Jew, then for the Gentile.

Colossians 1

3 We always thank God, the Father of our Lord Jesus Christ, when we pray for you,

4 because we have heard of your faith in Christ Jesus and of the love you have for all the saints--

5 the faith and love that spring from the hope that is stored up for you in heaven and that you have already heard about in the word of truth, the gospel

6 that has come to you. All over the world this gospel is bearing fruit and growing, just as it has been doing among you since the day you heard it and understood God's grace in all its truth.

7 You learned it from Epaphras, our dear fellow servant, who is a faithful minister of Christ on our behalf,

8 and who also told us of your love in the Spirit.

9 For this reason, since the day we heard about you, we have not stopped praying for you and asking God to fill you with the knowledge of his will through all spiritual wisdom and understanding.

Study Questions: Church Cooperation
Romans 1:8-14 & Colossians 1:3-9

Introduction:
Churches must work together to advance the kingdom of God. They are stronger and can do more when they support each other, encourage one another, and voluntarily work together as led by the Spirit. Although Paul has not been to Rome or met those at the church in Rome, the reputation of their faith had reached him. Paul is thankful for them and wants to visit them because he knows that it would be mutually encouraging. The Spirit of God and the Gospel of Jesus Christ has united them.

In the same way, the church in Colossae has been a part of the spread of the Gospel all over the world. They had learned about the Gospel from Epaphras, Paul's fellow servant. The churches had been encouraging one another, praying for each other, and united by the Spirit of God.

Grace Goals:
Knowledge
- To recognize the evidence of faith within a person.
- To know the power of God that comes through the Gospel to change lives.

Attitude
- To have confidence in the Gospel because of its saving power.
- To have a spirit of eagerness to share the gospel.

Actions
- To allow our faith in Jesus to change us so that it overflows and we can mutually encourage one another in the body.
- To work alongside other congregations for the sake of building up the kingdom of God.

Memory Verse:
Hebrews 10:24-25, And let us consider how we may spur one another on toward love and good deeds. Let us not give up meeting together, as some are in the habit of doing, but let us encourage one another – and all the more as you see the Day approaching.

Questions about the Text:

Romans 1

1. What was Paul thankful for from the church in Rome?
   (Romans 1:8 He was thankful for their faith and the testimony
   of their faith that was being reported around the world.)

2. What are some things that the beginning of this text says about
   faith? (Romans 1:8 Paul was thankful for the report of their
   faith. It was evident to the world, people were passing on the
   simple message of their faith and it brought glory to God.)

3. What was Paul's heart and attitude from the description of his
   prayers? (Romans 1:9-11 He was serving God in his spirit. His
   preaching was a part of who he was. He constantly prayed for
   those he had never met. He longed to see these believers and
   wanted to see them.)

4. What do these first verses teach us about God? (Romans 1:9-
   10 He is the one that Paul served. It was His Gospel and His
   Son. He is watching and listening at all times. He is the one
   that opens doors according to His will.)

5. How is the relationship between Paul and the Romans
   described? (Romans 1:9-12 He is praying for them. He is
   longing to see them so that He can give them a gift from the
   Spirit of God as well as be encouraged by them. They are a
   part of Paul's family because they shared the same faith and
   the same Father. They had been in his heart, his plans and his
   expected ministry. See 1 Timothy 4:14 and 2 Timothy 1:6)

6. Why does Paul say *that I might have a harvest among you*?
   (Romans 1:13 He is expecting people to come to faith, build
   each other up, and grow in the Lord together. Spiritual life and
   spiritual gifts are the fruit of what the Lord produces within
   people. See Acts 13:48 and 14:26-27)

7. What is the nature of Paul's obligation? (Romans 1:14 He
   describes it as a responsibility from God whom he serves, an
   obligation to God in preaching the Gospel of His Son and an
   obligation of love for God because he is eager to preach.)

Colossians 1

8. How does Paul's church and the Colossian church encourage
   each other? (Colossians 1:3-9 Paul is thankful to God for their

125

faith, love, and hope which is spreading all over the world. The Colossians are being encouraged by Paul's letter, his joy, the word of truth, his fellow partner Epaphras, and his prayers.)

9. What is the message that is being spread about the Colossians? (Colossians 1:4-5 They have faith in Jesus, love for the saints, hope in heaven, and they have heard the word of truth.)

10. How is the work of the Gospel described? (Colossians 1:6-7 It is bearing fruit, growing, being heard, and understood. The work was being done by a simple man, Epaphras who has been faithful in his role.)

11. What is the first thing Paul's church prays for the Colossian church? (Colossians 1:9 He prays that God would fill them with the knowledge of His will which comes through spiritual wisdom and understanding.)

Application Questions:
Romans 1

1. By whose faith and testimony are you encouraged? Has the message of that person spread to others as a testimony of what God can do?

2. What can you understand about your faith when you study this text? (Romans 1:8 Faith is a gift coming from God and we can only humbly receive it. When faith comes through Jesus, we have a person and facts on which to base our faith. Telling people about my faith encourages others and brings glory to God.)

3. How can we share in Paul's heart and attitude toward others? (Romans 1:9-11 When we pray for people, God changes our attitude toward them and unites our spirits. Mutual encouragement and the sharing of spiritual gifts can build a fellowship that longs to be together and feels like family.)

4. What can we thank God for as we look at this text? (Romans 1:8-12 We can be thankful for: the world wide church, the variety of spiritual gifts in people, those believing in Christ, those transformed by the Gospel and God's righteousness that comes by faith.)

5. What does this text describe as things that we can pray for others about? (Romans 1:10-14 We can pray for good fellowship and mutual encouragement, for spiritual fruit and more spiritual gifts, for opportunities to share the gospel, for the power of God and for righteousness that comes through faith.)

6. Where is God at work and how can we be a part of that? (Romans 1:8-14 God is at work wherever there is spiritual life, spiritual gifts, or someone is trusting Jesus. The Lord is at work in Christian fellowship, the preaching of the gospel, people being saved and the righteousness of God in a person's life.)

7. Are we obligated to anything like Paul was? (Romans 1:14 We have gifts and opportunities that come from God. We have the knowledge of the Gospel to share with others and we have a love for God because of what He has done. See Acts 20:26-27)

8. How can we bring the Gospel to those that think that the Gospel is foolish? How about those who think that they need to change before they come to Christ? (Romans 1:16 The Gospel is foolish to those that are perishing, but to those who are being saved it is the power of God. 1 Corinthians 1:18-31 The Gospel is the power of God that changes people. We cannot make ourselves good or civilized before coming to Christ.)

9. What type of power does the Gospel have for us today? (Romans 1:16 It has the same power today as it did when Paul wrote Romans. The good news of Jesus has the power of forgiveness of sins, of appeasing God, removing guilt, freedom from chains and addictions, conquering death, a way to heaven and a good life on this earth.)

10. How do we deal with the feeling of shame when we don't use opportunities to share the gospel? (Romans 1:16 We return to the promises of Scripture and we look at the power of the Gospel which has the power to change lives eternally. We must personally hear the Gospel and rest in God's forgiveness even when we daily sin against him.)

11. How can our churches encourage each other? (Colossians 1:4-6 We can also recognize the unique ministry roles that each church has. Different churches will be strong in different areas: outreach, Bible study, worship, community assistance, etc. Sharing the Word of God, notes of encouragement, talented leaders, and prayer for one another will build both churches up.)

12. What is the message that would be said about your church?

13. How is the Lord using the Gospel in your church? (Colossians 1:6-7 The Word of God will not return empty when it is shared with people. Not all of the effects are visible, but bearing fruit, growing, being heard, and understood are normal for any church regardless of the messenger.)

14. What does your church need prayer for? Which churches could be partnering together in prayer with you?

22. Church Discipleship
2 Timothy 1:1-14, 2:1-7

2 Timothy

1 Paul, an apostle of Christ Jesus by the will of God according to the promise of the life that is in Christ Jesus,

2 To Timothy, my beloved child:

Grace, mercy, and peace from God the Father and Christ Jesus our Lord.

3 I thank God whom I serve, as did my ancestors, with a clear conscience, as I remember you constantly in my prayers night and day.

4 As I remember your tears, I long to see you, that I may be filled with joy.

5 I am reminded of your sincere faith, a faith that dwelt first in your grandmother Lois and your mother Eunice and now, I am sure, dwells in you as well.

6 For this reason I remind you to fan into flame the gift of God, which is in you through the laying on of my hands,

7 for God gave us a spirit not of fear but of power and love and self-control.

8 Therefore do not be ashamed of the testimony about our Lord, nor of me his prisoner, but share in suffering for the gospel by the power of God,

9 who saved us and called us to a holy calling, not because of our works but because of his own purpose and grace, which he gave us in Christ Jesus before the ages began,

10 and which now has been manifested through the appearing of our Savior Christ Jesus, who abolished death and brought life and immortality to light through the gospel,

11 for which I was appointed a preacher and apostle and teacher,

12 which is why I suffer as I do. But I am not ashamed, for I know whom I have believed, and I am convinced that he is able to guard until that day what has been entrusted to me.

13 Follow the pattern of the sound words that you have heard from me, in the faith and love that are in Christ Jesus.

14 By the Holy Spirit who dwells within us, guard the good deposit entrusted to you.

2:1 You then, my child, be strengthened by the grace that is in Christ Jesus,

2 and what you have heard from me in the presence of many witnesses entrust to faithful men, who will be able to teach others also.

3 Share in suffering as a good soldier of Christ Jesus.

4 No soldier gets entangled in civilian pursuits, since his aim is to please the one who enlisted him.

5 An athlete is not crowned unless he competes according to the rules.

6 It is the hard-working farmer who ought to have the first share of the crops.

7 Think over what I say, for the Lord will give you understanding in everything.

Study Questions: Church Discipleship
2 Timothy 1:1-14, 2:1-7

Introduction:

The purpose of the church given in the Great Commission is to go and make disciples. Our churches today need to follow that instruction as much as the early church did. Paul's discipleship of Timothy is a great example of what that investment looks like. Paul met Timothy in Lystra. The son of a Jewish believing woman and a Greek father. Paul wanted Timothy to accompany him. As they went on their way through the cities, they strengthened the churches in the faith, so that they increased in numbers daily. The two of them traveled together, ministered together and then Paul entrusted the church of Ephesus into Timothy's care.

Grace Goals:

Knowledge
- – To know the power of God to carry out His calling.
- – To see the gifts of God that He places in our lives.

Attitude
- – To adopt people into our personal lives and mentor them.
- – To love those we are entrusted with.

Actions
- – To make disciples, who also make disciples.

Questions about the Text:

1. How does Paul view his relationship with Timothy? (2 Timothy 2:2-4 Timothy was like his own child. He was thankful to the Lord for him and prayed constantly for him. He longed to see him and be filled with joy.)

2. What was Paul's role in mentoring Timothy? (2 Timothy 2:3-6 Paul was actively investing in Timothy through his prayers, relationship, letters, and their common faith. Paul was advising Timothy, working alongside of him, and encouraging him.)

3. What role did his mother and grandmother have in teaching Timothy? (2 Timothy 2:5 They both had a sincere faith that was passed on from one generation to the next. The faith that Timothy had grown up with was now the faith that Paul continued to build on.)

4. How did the Lord work in Timothy? (2 Timothy 2:5-8 His faith came from the Lord as well as a gift of God. The Lord is the one who dispels fear and gives power, love, and self-control.)

5. What does Paul include in his description of ministry for Jesus? (2 Timothy 2:8-10 It included prison and suffering, yet the power of God was in the gospel. God is the one who saves us, calls us and sets us apart. He gives us work to do for His purpose and grace in Christ Jesus.)

6. What does Paul encourage Timothy to do? (2 Timothy 2:13-14 Follow the advice that Paul has told him. Listen to his teaching which comes from the faith and love in Christ Jesus. Allow the Holy Spirit to work in him, guarding what has been planted in him.)

7. Where does Timothy find the strength to carry out this responsibility? (2 Timothy 2:1 The grace of Christ Jesus is all the strength he needs.)

8. How is Timothy to pass on what he has received? (2 Timothy 2:2-3 That which he has received, he is to pass on to other faithful men, who will be able to teach others also. It is a continual disciple making process.)

9. What does Timothy have to look forward to? (2 Timothy 2:3-6 The ministry will include suffering. As a soldier his aim is to please his commanding officer. As an athlete his aim is compete according to the rules. As a farmer he will share in the joy of the harvest.)

Application Questions:
1. What are our mentoring relationships to look like? (2 Timothy 2:2-4 They are to be like the adoption of a person into our personal life. That means sharing the struggles, joys, prayers, and oneness in Christ.)

2. What is our role in mentoring people? (2 Timothy 2:3-6 We must invest ourselves to keep the relationship strong, but the bond that holds people together is faith in Jesus. He is the one that unites hearts in service to God.)

132

3. Who have been your spiritual parents and grandparents?

4. How has the Lord been at work in you? (2 Timothy 2:5-8 He is the one that begins the work by giving us faith. He gives us fruit of the Spirit and differing gifts. He is the one who dispels our fear and gives us power, love, and self-control.)

5. Do we share the challenges of ministry as well as the joys? (2 Timothy 2:8-10 Ministry will be difficult as long as we live on earth. The challenges are both external as well as internal. However, it is still God who saves us, calls us and sets us apart. He gives us work to do for His purpose and grace in Christ Jesus.)

6. What advice would you give to the one you mentor? (2 Timothy 2:13-14 Paul does give Timothy advice, but it is always based on that which is in Jesus and through the power of the Holy Spirit.)

7. Where do you need strength in the grace of Christ Jesus?

8. To whom can you pass on what you have received?

9. What motivations can keep you focused in ministry?

23. Church Discipline
Matthew 18:15-35

15 "If your brother sins against you, go and show him his fault, just between the two of you. If he listens to you, you have won your brother over.

16 But if he will not listen, take one or two others along, so that 'every matter may be established by the testimony of two or three witnesses.'

17 If he refuses to listen to them, tell it to the church; and if he refuses to listen even to the church, treat him as you would a pagan or a tax collector.

18 "I tell you the truth, whatever you bind on earth will be bound in heaven, and whatever you loose on earth will be loosed in heaven.

19 "Again, I tell you that if two of you on earth agree about anything you ask for, it will be done for you by my Father in heaven.

20 For where two or three come together in my name, there am I with them."

21 Then Peter came to Jesus and asked, "Lord, how many times shall I forgive my brother when he sins against me? Up to seven times?"

22 Jesus answered, "I tell you, not seven times, but seventy-seven times.

23 "Therefore, the kingdom of heaven is like a king who wanted to settle accounts with his servants.

24 As he began the settlement, a man who owed him ten thousand talents was brought to him.

25 Since he was not able to pay, the master ordered that he and his wife and his children and all that he had be sold to repay the debt.

26 "The servant fell on his knees before him. 'Be patient with me,' he begged, 'and I will pay back everything.'

27 The servant's master took pity on him, canceled the debt and let him go.

28 "But when that servant went out, he found one of his fellow servants who owed him a hundred denarii. He grabbed him and began to choke him. 'Pay back what you owe me!' he demanded.

29 "His fellow servant fell to his knees and begged him, 'Be patient with me, and I will pay you back.'

30 "But he refused. Instead, he went off and had the man thrown into prison until he could pay the debt.

31 When the other servants saw what had happened, they were greatly distressed and went and told their master everything that had happened.

32 "Then the master called the servant in. 'You wicked servant,' he said, 'I canceled all that debt of yours because you begged me to.

33 Shouldn't you have had mercy on your fellow servant just as I had on you?'

34 In anger his master turned him over to the jailers to be tortured, until he should pay back all he owed.

35 "This is how my heavenly Father will treat each of you unless you forgive your brother from your heart."

Study Questions: Church Discipline
Matthew 18:15-35

Introduction:
It is the responsibility of the church to purify itself by correcting and confronting those who are living in sin.

Every day people do bad things to us. It may be in their actions, their words or the thoughts of their minds. They might say bad things about us, show us disrespect, talk wrongly about us, steal things, etc. In the same way, we also do things that are hurtful to people around us. Although it is easy to feel anger and hatred toward someone who wrongs us, we can easily forget how many times and how many ways we have sinned against God. There is no way to compare the small number of sins that others do against us in comparison to the uncountable number of things we do against God. Because the Lord forgives us all of our sins, we also can forgive others their sins against us.

Grace Goals:
Knowledge
- To know that we have sinned more than we can count because our nature is rebellious toward God.
- To know that God is gracious and forgives the sins of those who repent and ask His forgiveness.

Attitude
- To honor God as your King who is to be respected as the highest authority.
- To rely on God's forgiveness for our every sin.
- To be humble and forgiving toward other people.

Action
- To ask forgiveness from those that we have sinned against.
- To forgive others for their sins against you. This forgiveness includes getting rid of bitterness in your heart.

Memory Verse:
James 5:16 "Therefore confess your sins to each other and pray for each other so that you may be healed. The prayer of a righteous man is powerful and effective."

Questions about the Story:
1. What did Jesus tell Peter about how many times he must forgive his brother? (Matthew 18:21-22 Jesus replied that Peter shouldn't forgive his brother only 7 times, but 77 times.

This was meant to show Peter that the number of times we forgive should be beyond counting.)

2. What was Jesus describing in this story? (Matthew 18:23, 35 The Kingdom of Heaven where God is the just and merciful king and an unforgiving person is like the selfish, greedy servant. The debt is our sin against God and against one another.)

3. What did the servant who owed the king 10,000 talents ask the king to do? (Matthew 18:26 The servant pleaded with the king for mercy, patience, and time to repay the debt; which was equal to 200,000 years of wages. One talent equaled 20 years of labor.)

4. What was the king's response? (Matthew 18:27 The king showed forgiveness by canceling the servant's huge debt and by allowing him to go free.)

5. How does the servant's response after his release show his character? (Matthew 18:28-30 His demand for repayment, his aggressive attack, his refusal to show mercy and his throwing the servant into prison shows an inner character that was not changed by receiving mercy himself.)

6. Why did the king reverse his decision to forgive the first servant his great debt? (Matthew 18:32-33 The king could see that the first servant did not learn by receiving mercy and did not appreciate the mercy he had received. So the king in anger delivered him to the jailers.)

7. Why did the king have the jailers torture the first servant? (Matthew 18:34 Instead of the mercy that the king desired to show, the servant showed that his heart was hard.)

8. How do the two debts compare to one another? (Matthew 18:24, 28 The second debt is insignificant compared to the first debt. The second debt was equal to 100 days wages.)

9. What will happen to us if we don't genuinely forgive other people? (Matthew 18:35 We will receive from God Almighty the same kind of punishment as the wicked servant got.)

Application Questions:

1. How many times must we forgive other people? What must we forgive them for? Why? (Matthew 18:21-22 We must forgive others people whenever they do wrong to us, because our Heavenly Father has forgiven the un-payable debt that we owe Him because of our sin. Luke 11:4; Ephesians 4:31-32)

2. Where is the kingdom of heaven? (Anywhere that God is King and Lord. It begins now in the lives of those who are His children by faith, and will be completed and made perfect in heaven.)

3. If the Lord was going to settle accounts with us, how would we come out? (Matthew 18:23 In our own nature, we would be nothing but indebted sinners.)

4. What do we need to do about the debt that we owe to God for our sins? (Matthew 18:26: We need to come before the Lord to plead for forgiveness for our sins. Jesus is the one that took the punishment that we deserved upon Himself, and God says He is faithful and just to forgive us if we confess our sins to Him. John 1:9)

5. What will God do for us when we ask Him for mercy and forgiveness? How many times will He do this? (Matthew 18:27 In His great love and mercy, the Lord is always ready to forgive our sins when we confess them and repent. He cleans us by the blood of the Lord Jesus, who carried our sins in His body when He died on the cross. This pays the debt that we owe Him, and so our account with God is paid.)

6. What types of sins from other people are difficult to forgive? What is our attitude toward people that have hurt us and wronged us?

7. What would the King say to us if He were to see how we treat the people around us?

8. What is the warning for us if we don't forgive others? (Matthew 18:35 If we don't forgive other people around us, our Heavenly Father will not forgive us. He who has been forgiven little loves little, Luke 7:36-50.)

9. Are there people in your life whom you have not forgiven? (Matthew 6:12-15, Colossians 3:12-13)

10. How much has God forgiven us? (Romans 5:8 While we were still sinners, Christ died for us, also Colossians 3:13.)

24. Church Finances
1 Corinthians 16:1-11 & Luke 21:1-4

1 Corinthians 16
1 Now about the collection for God's people: Do what I told the Galatian churches to do.
2 On the first day of every week, each one of you should set aside a sum of money in keeping with his income, saving it up, so that when I come no collections will have to be made.
3 Then, when I arrive, I will give letters of introduction to the men you approve and send them with your gift to Jerusalem.
4 If it seems advisable for me to go also, they will accompany me.
5 After I go through Macedonia, I will come to you-- for I will be going through Macedonia.
6 Perhaps I will stay with you awhile, or even spend the winter, so that you can help me on my journey, wherever I go.
7 I do not want to see you now and make only a passing visit; I hope to spend some time with you, if the Lord permits.
8 But I will stay on at Ephesus until Pentecost,
9 because a great door for effective work has opened to me, and there are many who oppose me.
10 When Timothy comes, see to it that he has nothing to fear while he is with you, for he is carrying on the work of the Lord, just as I am.
11 No one, then, should treat him with contempt. Send him on his way in peace so that he may return to me. I am expecting him along with the brothers.

Luke 21
1 As he looked up, Jesus saw the rich putting their gifts into the temple treasury.
2 He also saw a poor widow put in two very small copper coins.
3 "I tell you the truth," he said, "this poor widow has put in more than all the others.
4 All these people gave their gifts out of their wealth; but she out of her poverty put in all she had to live on."

Study Questions: Church Finances
1 Corinthians 16:1-11 & Luke 21:1-4

Introduction:
Congregations are mutually lifted up through their partnership in achieving things that are greater than what an individual church can do and especially more than a single individual. One way that they can work together is through helping those of God's people who are in need. Another way is to join together to support those who take God's Word to others. It is important to work together to train men for the ministry, distribute Bibles and Christian literature, plant churches, send missionaries and to carry out acts of mercy.

Grace Goals:
Knowledge
- To consider how churches can work together for the Lord's work.

Attitude
- To have compassion for those in need.
- To show love to those who lead the ministries of the church.

Actions
- To raise the support to meet the needs of God's people.
- To provide for those that are serving the Lord full-time.
- To pray that the Lord would guide you in your tithe.

Questions about the Text:
1 Corinthians 16
1. What is the purpose of the collection? (1 Corinthians 16:1 It is for God's people and specifically those in Jerusalem.)

2. What instructions are they to follow regarding these finances? (1 Corinthians 16:1-2 The contribution should be planned for, set aside, saved and match the person's income. The same instructions were also given to other churches.)

3. How will the money be handled? (1 Corinthians 16:3-4 The congregation will decide on men who will take the money to Jerusalem.)

4. How have Paul and the church in Corinth been working together? (1 Corinthians 16:5-7 Paul has been a traveling missionary on their behalf. He comes and stays with them,

then he is sent out. His ministry through their church has reached into Macedonia and the many places that Paul has gone. He is also ministering to them and desires to spend time with them.)

5. What directs the affairs of Paul's ministry? (1 Corinthians 16:1, 7-9 Paul notes that the collection is for God's people and He hopes to spend time in Corinth "if the Lord permits." The Lord is the one who opens great doors for effective ministry even though there maybe those that oppose him.)

6. What is Timothy's role in ministry? (1 Corinthians 16:10-11 He was carrying on "the work of the Lord" like Paul was. Timothy had been assigned as a pastor over the church in Ephesus. See 1 Timothy 1:3 He was also a support for Paul and a connection for him to the church.)

Luke 21
7. Who and what was it that Jesus saw? (Luke 21:1 & 2 Jesus saw a people who were rich and a poor woman giving their tithe at a temple. Malachi 3:10 and Deut. 14:22 describe the tithe.)

8. According to what Jesus said who put more into the temple treasury? (Luke 21:3 The poor woman who only put in two small copper coins.)

9. Again, according to Jesus what was it that the poor woman actually gave? (Luke 21:4 She gave out of her poverty which shows and reveals her trust in the Lord and His promises to her.

Application Questions:
1. Why do we take an offering at church? (1 Corinthians 16:1 There are many expenses that church is responsible for, but the beginning of that is for God's people who are in need which includes those leading the ministry.)

2. What are some biblical ways to handle our finances? (1 Corinthians 16:1-2 We also need to set aside our money for the work of the Lord. We need to do it regularly, voluntarily, in keeping with our income.)

142

3. How should the finances in the church be handled?
   (1 Corinthians 16:3-4 The church should choose men who will
   be in charge of giving the money to where it is intended to go.
   People that can be trusted and can verify it is handled well.)

4. Who does your congregation support as a missionary to take
   God's Word to people far away? (1 Corinthians 16:5-7 Every
   church needs to see themselves as a missionary sending
   church. They may not be able to support one individual on
   their own, but they work with other churches to send
   someone.)

5. How does your church know what to do? (1 Corinthians 16:1,
   7-9 The church is the Lord's and it must serve Him first. That
   includes His people, the spread of His kingdom, and His
   effective doors of ministry.)

6. Is your pastor supported by the church? (1 Corinthians 16:10-
   11 They carry on the work of the Lord like missionaries. They
   are the link between the church and God's people.)

7. What should be our attitude towards the resources that we
   have? (We should acknowledge that it is the Lord that owns
   all and it is Him that promises that we will be taken care of but
   that we are called to be faithful stewards of what God has
   entrusted to us.)

8. What responsibility do we individually have towards the needs
   of our churches and the needs around us? (God has called us
   and chosen us to be the ones to spread His Word and to be the
   ones to even finance the projects ahead of us.)

25. Churches Mission
Acts 11:19-26 & Acts 13:1-3

Acts 11

[19]Now those who had been scattered by the persecution in connection with Stephen traveled as far as Phoenicia, Cyprus and Antioch, telling the message only to Jews. [20]Some of them, however, men from Cyprus and Cyrene, went to Antioch and began to speak to Greeks also, telling them the good news about the Lord Jesus. [21]The Lord's hand was with them, and a great number of people believed and turned to the Lord.

[22]News of this reached the ears of the church at Jerusalem, and they sent Barnabas to Antioch. [23]When he arrived and saw the evidence of the grace of God, he was glad and encouraged them all to remain true to the Lord with all their hearts. [24]He was a good man, full of the Holy Spirit and faith, and a great number of people were brought to the Lord.

[25]Then Barnabas went to Tarsus to look for Saul, [26]and when he found him, he brought him to Antioch. So for a whole year Barnabas and Saul met with the church and taught great numbers of people. The disciples were called Christians first at Antioch.

Acts 13

1 In the church at Antioch there were prophets and teachers. Barnabas, Simeon called Niger, Lucius of Cyrene, Manaen (who had been brought up with Herod the tetrarch) and Saul.

2 While they were worshiping the Lord and fasting, the Holy Spirit said, "Set apart for me Barnabas and Saul for the work to which I have called them."

3 So after they had fasted and prayed, they placed their hands on them and sent them off.

Study Questions: Churches Mission
Acts 11:19-26 & Acts 13:1-3

Introduction:

Churches must work together to reach out to unbelievers. In this text there are people from several towns sharing the good news of the Lord Jesus. The city of Antioch was a large compared to Jerusalem, so when the "ears of the church at Jerusalem" heard of the large numbers of people being brought to the Lord, they immediately sent Barnabas to find out what was going on. Barnabas realized he needed help, so he went to Tarsus to find Paul so they could work together in this new mission field.

We see in Acts 13 that it was the responsibility of the church to call and send workers to spread the Gospel. It is the church that the Holy Spirit used to choose Paul and Barnabas and it was the church that fasted, prayed and sent out the missionaries.

Grace Goals:

Knowledge
- To realize how many people around the world need the word.
- To consider how simple sharing the word can be.

Attitude
- To allow the evidence of God's grace to shine.
- To let the Holy Spirit encourage people through us.

Actions
- To participate in God's kingdom mission for all people.
- To share the good news of the Lord Jesus.

Questions about the Story:

Acts 11

1. How did the Lord use the persecution? (Acts 11:19-21 He used it to get the people out sharing with others.)

2. Who was the message going out to? (Acts 11:19-21 They were telling the good news about Jesus Christ first to the Jews, but then also to the Greeks. Great numbers believed and turned to the Lord. It was an enormous cultural shift to bring the message to the Greeks.)

3. What was the result of God's Word going out into the world? (Acts 11:21-23 "Great numbers of people believed and turned to the Lord." People were being saved and their lives

displayed "the evidence of the grace of God." The living Word was changing lives.)

4. How is Barnabas' described? (Acts 11:24 Barnabas is described as a good man, full of the Holy Spirit and faith. These attributes come from the work of God in his life. His life also displayed the fruit of God; "great numbers of people were brought to the Lord.")

5. What does it mean to be full of the Holy Spirit? (That the Holy Spirit is living inside you and working through you.)

6. Why did Barnabas go to look for Saul? (Acts 11:25-26 He looked for Saul in order to bring him back to Antioch and help with the ministry. Barnabas needed Saul because he was unique; he was from both the Jewish and the Roman cultures and could teach well.)

7. What is significant about Barnabas and Saul teaching for a whole year? (Acts 11:26 It is the Word of God that changes lives and it is the Word of God that strengthened those new believers. It is the foundation of faith. Romans 10:17 says, "faith comes by hearing the message, and the message is heard through the Word of Christ.")

Acts 13
8. Who was meeting together and who spoke to them? (Acts 13:1 & 2 The prophets and teachers of the church in Antioch were meeting together and the Holy Spirit spoke to them.)

9. What was the church active in doing before the Holy Spirit spoke to them? (The church was there worshiping the Lord and fasting.)

10. Who was set aside and what were they set aside for? (They set aside Barnabas and Saul to carry out the work that the Holy Spirit called them to do.)

11. What was the reaction of the church? (They continued to fast and pray and then they laid their hands on Barnabas and Saul, prayed over them and sent them out.)

12.

Application Questions:

1. In what situations should we sharing the Word of God with other people? (Acts 11:19-20; Anytime can be a time to be sharing it with others. Whether you are walking down the road or in an unfamiliar land.)

2. Who are the untouchable Greeks of our day? (Acts 11:19-21 There are many that we label as outside of the kingdom of God, but the good news of the Lord Jesus is for all of them.)

3. What power enables us to go out? (Acts 11:21 The Holy Spirit and the Word of God are the power and the authority.)

4. Can people tell that you have been changed and that God has turned you around? What do they see in your life? (Acts 11:22, 26 The evidence of the grace of God is as visible as your changed life.)

5. In what ways can we remain true to the Lord with all of our heart? (Acts 11:23 The Word of God, prayer and the fellowship of believers help us grow in the Lord.)

6. Why is it important to have a partner in ministry? (Acts 11:25-26 Other people's gifts can complement what the Lord has given us.)

7. When can we be learning from others and to whom can we be teaching the Word of God? (Acts 11:26 There are Christians that can teach us the Word of God as it has applies to our lives. There are also many people that need to know the Word of God that we can teach.)

8. What part should a church have in missions? (They should be actively worshiping the Lord and submitting to the Holy Spirit. They should also be obedient in sending their members out for the sake of mission work home and abroad.)

9. How is your church active in mission work (planting churches and sending people to new areas for ministry)?

Leaders

Lessons 26-34

26.   The Character
Titus 1:4-9

Titus 1

4 To Titus, my true son in our common faith: Grace and peace from God the Father and Christ Jesus our Savior.

5 The reason I left you in Crete was that you might straighten out what was left unfinished and appoint elders in every town, as I directed you.

6 An elder must be blameless, the husband of but one wife, a man whose children believe and are not open to the charge of being wild and disobedient.

7 Since an overseer is entrusted with God's work, he must be blameless-- not overbearing, not quick-tempered, not given to drunkenness, not violent, not pursuing dishonest gain.

8 Rather he must be hospitable, one who loves what is good, who is self-controlled, upright, holy and disciplined.

9 He must hold firmly to the trustworthy message as it has been taught, so that he can encourage others by sound doctrine and refute those who oppose it.

1 Timothy 3:1-13

1 Here is a trustworthy saying: Whoever aspires to be an overseer desires a noble task. 2 Now the overseer is to be above reproach, faithful to his wife, temperate, self-controlled, respectable, hospitable, able to teach, 3 not given to drunkenness, not violent but gentle, not quarrelsome, not a lover of money. 4 He must manage his own family well and see that his children obey him, and he must do so in a manner worthy of full respect. 5 (If anyone does not know how to manage his own family, how can he take care of God's church?) 6 He must not be a recent convert, or he may become conceited and fall under the same judgment as the devil. 7 He must also have a good reputation with outsiders, so that he will not fall into disgrace and into the devil's trap. 8 In the same way, deacons are to be worthy of respect, sincere, not indulging in much wine, and not pursuing dishonest gain. 9 They must keep hold of the deep truths of the faith with a clear conscience. 10 They must first be tested; and then if there is nothing against them, let them serve as deacons.

11 In the same way, the women are to be worthy of respect, not malicious talkers but temperate and trustworthy in everything.

12 A deacon must be faithful to his wife and must manage his children and his household well. 13 Those who have served well gain an excellent standing and great assurance in their faith in Christ Jesus.

Study Questions: The Character
Titusl:4-9

Introduction:
A church needs organization and that starts with its leaders. The character that is in its leaders will become the character by which the church is known. The challenge of finding good leaders is just as true today as it was for the early church. It is important to note that any positive character and outward qualities that a person displays is a reflection of the work of God in their life rather than a natural attribute in themselves. The description that Titus uses regarding the Cretans is enough to highlight the contrast between the natural man and godly character.

Grace Goals:

Knowledge
  - To realize the importance of character in the life of church leaders.
  - To see the outward fruits of the Holy Spirits work in a person.

Attitude
  - To desire to grow in godly qualities with the Spirits help.
  - To respect those that have been entrusted with leadership.

Actions
  - To choose responsible leaders for the church.
  - To display these godly qualities of leadership, by God's grace.

Questions about the Text:

1. What does Paul's greeting of sonship say about his relationship with Titus? (Titus 1:4 Paul's greeting to Titus as a "true son in our common faith" is a picture of the close bond that they share. Their faith and ministry for the Lord has united them.)

2. Why does Paul greet Titus with grace and peace? (Titus 1:4 Grace and peace are primary needs for anyone in ministry. It is the grace of God that creates a pastor out of a pagan. It is the grace of God that is at work in the difficult people he is left to "straighten out." It is the peace of God that gives him the perseverance to see the task through It is the grace and peace of God that is the heart of the message for the pastor to

proclaim.)

3. Why does it matter that the grace and peace come from "God the Father and Christ Jesus our Savior?" (Titus 1:4 It is the Father who is in charge. Since He is ruling over all things, then peace is possible. It is Jesus who is the Savior. He is the one that makes the grace possible.)

4. What is the primary responsibility given to Titus? (Titus 1:5 He is entrusted with appointing elders. Paul's statement, "straighten out what was left unfinished" is the first picture into what is described in the chapter. Appointing elders in Crete was a challenging task because Creatans were described as "liars, evil beasts, lazy gluttons." It is no wonder that Titus needed grace and peace.)

5. What do the three qualities of the elder say about the man? (Titus 1:6 They mean that he has been able to maintain personal self-control, has worked out differences between himself and his wife, and has managed his children wisely. These three do not mean that he is perfect. They mean that he has used wisdom in handling his home affairs and could be trusted with the family of God.)

6. What does the overseer list reveal? (Titus 1:7-8)
   a. blameless – maintained a good reputation before people
   b. not overbearing – externally self-controlled, able to hear what others say rather than being controlling
   c. not quick-tempered – internally self-controlled regarding things that don't meet his expectations
   d. not given to drunkenness – control over inward lusts or pleasures
   e. not violent – control over outward anger or passions
   f. not pursuing dishonest gain – content with what the Lord provides
   g. hospitable – welcoming to others, sharing what he has
   h. loves what is good – an outward display of the inner desire
   i. self-controlled – may be better described as spirit-controlled.
   j. upright – honorable and honest

      k.   holy – set apart for ministry, not distracted by the world.

      l.   disciplined – personally watchful of their behavior

7.   How is this list possible for anyone? (Titus 1:9 It might be possible to think of areas of success on the list, but no one is qualified in themselves. The text says hold firmly to the trustworthy message, which is the Gospel of Jesus, His grace and His peace.)

Application Questions:

1.   How do we feel about fellow workers in ministry? (Titus 1:4 There is a sense of family within the Christian faith, but there can be an even deeper bond between two leaders who serve together.)

2.   When do we need grace and peace for our ministry? (Titus 1:4 We certainly need it personally because of our own failures, but those that we serve also need it. We need to know God's peace when the challenges of ministry are out of our control.)

3.   How does God the Father and Jesus the Son bring stability to our life? (Titus 1:4 Regardless of injustices that happen, the Father has the last word. Everyone will give an account to Him. Jesus has made heaven possible and so the trials of this world will all fade away in light of eternity.)

4.   What responsibilities do we have as members of God's church? (Titus 1:5 We must elect or appoint godly leaders who will manage the affairs of the church well. We also must be those leaders who the Lord uses for His kingdom work.)

5.   What is your reputation regarding your life, your spouse, and your children? (Titus 1:6 Those closest to us are the ones able to describe most clearly how our life is really going.)

6.   What from this list has the Lord already been working on in you and what areas still need work? (Titus 1:7-8

      a.   blameless –

      b.   not overbearing –

      c.   not quick-tempered –

      d.   not given to drunkenness –

      e.   not violent –

      f.   not pursuing dishonest gain –

g. hospitable –
h. loves what is good –
i. self-controlled –
j. upright –
k. holy –
l. disciplined –

7. How has the trustworthy message encouraged you or kept you in life and ministry? (Titus 1:9)

27. The Selection
Acts 6:1-8

Acts 6

1 In those days when the number of disciples was increasing, the Grecian Jews among them complained against the Hebraic Jews because their widows were being overlooked in the daily distribution of food.

2 So the Twelve gathered all the disciples together and said, "It would not be right for us to neglect the ministry of the word of God in order to wait on tables.

3 Brothers, choose seven men from among you who are known to be full of the Spirit and wisdom. We will turn this responsibility over to them

4 and will give our attention to prayer and the ministry of the word."

5 This proposal pleased the whole group. They chose Stephen, a man full of faith and of the Holy Spirit; also Philip, Procorus, Nicanor, Timon, Parmenas, and Nicolas from Antioch, a convert to Judaism.

6 They presented these men to the apostles, who prayed and laid their hands on them.

7 So the word of God spread. The number of disciples in Jerusalem increased rapidly, and a large number of priests became obedient to the faith.

8 Now Stephen, a man full of God's grace and power, did great wonders and miraculous signs among the people.

Introduction:
The people must choose leaders whom they trust to direct their church, preach God's Word, and care for them. The pastor or leaders are only people. They are no different from anyone else in the congregation except for the fact that they have been chosen and they have been entrusted to direct the affairs of the church. They are given the privilege and the responsibility to preach the word and care for the people. It is a task that any man would be completely inadequate to perform in themselves, but the Holy Spirit is the one that fills them with God's grace and power.

Grace Goals:
Knowledge
  – To see the need for men dedicated to run the church.
  – To understand the leader's need for the Holy Spirit's power.

Attitude
  – To unite behind the leaders of our church.
  – To respect our leaders.

Actions
  – To carefully choose and support the churches' leaders.

Questions about the Text:
1. Why was there a need to choose additional people to help lead the church? (Acts 6:1 The number of disciples was increasing, there were specific tasks that needed close attention, and the apostles needed to focus their time on prayer and ministry of the word.)

2. How did the apostles solve the problem? (Acts 6:2-3 They presented the matter to all of the disciples and let them be a part of the solution. The men that were chosen came from the greater body of disciples rather than being appointed by the apostles.)

3. What character qualities were the disciples looking for? (Acts 6:3 They were to be full of the Holy Spirit and wisdom. Full of faith was another description given to Stephen, but it was not a long list of requirements.)

4. How was the selection carried out? (Acts 6:5 It says that the proposal pleased the whole group, which describes a group consciences. The details of the selection are not given, but they presented the seven men to the apostles for commissioning and prayer.)

5. What was the result of this new assignment and selection? (Acts 6:7 It simply says that the Word of God spread and the number of disciples in Jerusalem increased rapidly. The responsibility that they carried was only the distribution of food, but the result was the multiplication of ministry.)

6. How is Stephen described in this new position? (Acts 6:8 He is given a description that equates with the apostles. His role became far greater than his initial responsibility. He is described as a man full of God's grace and power, who did great wonders and miraculous signs. This new position pushed him forward to do great things for the Lord.)

7. What does the text say about the man named Nicolas? How does this relate to 1 Timothy 3:6? (The text says that he was a convert from Judaism. First, in Acts it doesn't say that he was or was not a resent convert and either way he was set aside not as a deacon or an elder but as one to take care of the physical needs.)

Application Questions:
1. When does a church need to choose additional people? (Acts 6:1 When a church increases in size it is difficult for the needs of all the people to be met by only a few leaders. A house church may only need one or two leaders, but a larger church needs more leaders to care for the people.)

2. Who should make the selection for the leadership of the church? (Acts 6:2-3 Those who are participating in the church should be the ones directing the church. That gives the people ownership in the direction or affairs of the church.)

3. What character qualities should the pastor of our churches have? (Acts 6:3 We tend to make a long list of requirements for our pastor and leaders. The first critical quality is that they are full of the Holy Spirit, who can make up for any personal weaknesses. The second quality is wisdom which is the ability to apply the Word of God to their lives.)

4. How should we choose our pastors? (Acts 6:5 It should be a group consciences so that "it pleases the whole group" and it needs to be a matter of prayer. When a person has been selected, there needs to be a time when they are presented to the congregation for commissioning and prayer.)

5. Will the church increase rapidly like it did for the disciples in Jerusalem? (Acts 6:7 This is not a formula for church growth. However, when the responsibility for ministry is entrusted to people who can minister full-time, then they do have more time to spread the Word of God or they are able to remove roadblocks for ministry growth.)

6. What is the Holy Spirit's role with regard to raising up leaders? (Acts 6:8 Like with Stephen, the Holy Spirit can equip the person that is called far beyond what they are able to do in and of themselves. The description given to Stephen highlights "God's grace and power" rather than his own abilities.)

7. As we look at the fact that Nicolas was a Jewish convert; how are we reaching out to the lost and building them up for leadership within our churches?

28. The Call
Jeremiah 1:4-10 & Jonah 1-4

Jeremiah 1

[4] The word of the LORD came to me, saying,

[5] "Before I formed you in the womb I knew you,
  before you were born I set you apart;
  I appointed you as a prophet to the nations."

[6] "Ah, Sovereign LORD," I said, "I do not know how to speak; I am only a child."

[7] But the LORD said to me, "Do not say, 'I am only a child.' You must go to everyone I send you to and say whatever I command you. [8] Do not be afraid of them, for I am with you and will rescue you," declares the LORD.

[9] Then the LORD reached out his hand and touched my mouth and said to me, "Now, I have put my words in your mouth.

[10] See, today I appoint you over nations and kingdoms to uproot and tear down, to destroy and overthrow, to build and to plant."

Jonah 1

[1] The word of the LORD came to Jonah son of Amittai: [2] "Go to the great city of Nineveh and preach against it, because its wickedness has come up before me."

[3] But Jonah ran away from the LORD and headed for Tarshish. He went down to Joppa, where he found a ship bound for that port. After paying the fare, he went aboard and sailed for Tarshish to flee from the LORD.

[4] Then the LORD sent a great wind on the sea, and such a violent storm arose that the ship threatened to break up. [5] All the sailors were afraid and each cried out to his own god. And they threw the cargo into the sea to lighten the ship. But Jonah had gone below deck, where he lay down and fell into a deep sleep. [6] The captain went to him and said, "How can you sleep? Get up and call on your god! Maybe he will take notice of us, and we will not perish."

[7] Then the sailors said to each other, "Come, let us cast lots to find out who is responsible for this calamity." They cast lots and the lot fell on Jonah. [8] So they asked him, "Tell us, who is responsible for making all this trouble for us? What do you do? Where do you come from? What is your country? From what people are you?" [9] He answered, "I am a Hebrew and I worship the LORD, the God of heaven, who made the sea and the land."

[10] This terrified them and they asked, "What have you done?" (They knew he was running away from the LORD, because he had already told them so.) [11] The sea was getting rougher and rougher. So they

asked him, "What should we do to you to make the sea calm down for us?" ¹² "Pick me up and throw me into the sea," he replied, "and it will become calm. I know that it is my fault that this great storm has come upon you."
¹³ Instead, the men did their best to row back to land. But they could not, for the sea grew even wilder than before. ¹⁴ Then they cried to the LORD, "O LORD, please do not let us die for taking this man's life. Do not hold us accountable for killing an innocent man, for you, O LORD, have done as you pleased." ¹⁵ Then they took Jonah and threw him overboard, and the raging sea grew calm. ¹⁶ At this the men greatly feared the LORD, and they offered a sacrifice to the LORD and made vows to him.
¹⁷ But the LORD provided a great fish to swallow Jonah, and Jonah was inside the fish three days and three nights.

Jonah 2
¹ From inside the fish Jonah prayed to the LORD his God. ² He said: "In my distress I called to the LORD, and he answered me. From the depths of the grave I called for help, and you listened to my cry.
¹⁰ And the LORD commanded the fish, and it vomited Jonah onto dry land.

Jonah 3
¹ Then the word of the LORD came to Jonah a second time: ² "Go to the great city of Nineveh and proclaim to it the message I give you."
³ Jonah obeyed the word of the LORD and went to Nineveh. Now Nineveh was a very important city—a visit required three days. ⁴ On the first day, Jonah started into the city. He proclaimed: "Forty more days and Nineveh will be overturned." ⁵ The Ninevites believed God. They declared a fast, and all of them, from the greatest to the least, put on sackcloth.
⁶ When the news reached the king of Nineveh, he rose from his throne, took off his royal robes, covered himself with sackcloth and sat down in the dust.
¹⁰ When God saw what they did and how they turned from their evil ways, he had compassion and did not bring upon them the destruction he had threatened.

Jonah 4
¹ But Jonah was greatly displeased and became angry. ² He prayed to the LORD, "O LORD, is this not what I said when I was still at home? That is why I was so quick to flee to Tarshish. I knew that you are a gracious and compassionate God, slow to anger and abounding in love,

a God who relents from sending calamity. [3] Now, O LORD, take away my life, for it is better for me to die than to live."

[4] But the LORD replied, "Have you any right to be angry?"

[5] Jonah went out and sat down at a place east of the city. There he made himself a shelter, sat in its shade and waited to see what would happen to the city. [6] Then the LORD God provided a vine and made it grow up over Jonah to give shade for his head to ease his discomfort, and Jonah was very happy about the vine. [7] But at dawn the next day God provided a worm, which chewed the vine so that it withered. [8] When the sun rose, God provided a scorching east wind, and the sun blazed on Jonah's head so that he grew faint. He wanted to die, and said, "It would be better for me to die than to live."

[9] But God said to Jonah, "Do you have a right to be angry about the vine?" "I do," he said. "I am angry enough to die." [10] But the LORD said, "You have been concerned about this vine, though you did not tend it or make it grow. It sprang up overnight and died overnight. [11] But Nineveh has more than a hundred and twenty thousand people who cannot tell their right hand from their left, and many cattle as well. Should I not be concerned about that great city?"

Study Questions: The Call
Jeremiah 1:4-10 & Jonah 1-4

Introduction:
At times the call of God is difficult to accept or understand. The tasks that the Lord asks us to do seem far beyond our ability. It is true that God's plans for us may seem impossible, but nothing is impossible for God. So, even our weaknesses and fears make the greatness of God that much more amazing. The Lord is able to use us for His glory, because He is the one doing the work.

As a young person Jeremiah received a call to do the Lord's work. It was more than he felt capable of doing, but Jeremiah had been created and called for the Lord's work and the Lord carried him to the end. The Lord also called Jonah to be His prophet, but Jonah refused. Instead, he tried to run away and had to face the consequences. For both Jeremiah and Jonah, the Lord kept His promises and He used them to proclaim His Word.

Grace Goals:
Knowledge
- To know that God does have a plan for our lives, even though we can't see it, understand it or even feel capable for it.
- To understand that we cannot hide from God and the consequences are unpleasant.

Attitude
- To trust the Lord and His faithfulness. He can use us to do exceedingly, abundantly beyond all we could ask or think.
- To be willing and humble servants.

Actions
- To patiently seek the Lord's direction for our lives.
- To obey the Lord's call without question.

Memory Verse:
Exodus 4:11-12 "The LORD said to him, 'Who gave man his mouth? Who makes him deaf or mute? Who gives him sight or makes him blind? Is it not I, the LORD? Now go; I will help you speak and will teach you what to say.'"

Questions about the Text:
Jeremiah
1. What is significant about Jeremiah's call? (Jeremiah 1:4-10 The Word of God came to him and told him that he had

been created, set apart, appointed and directed for the Lord's work. The Lord told him what to say and do.)

2. Why is it important that the LORD predestined Jeremiah before he was born? (Jeremiah 1:5 The LORD had been planning his life and was directing him. Jeremiah could be confident in the Lord regardless of his age or his fears.)

3. What does Jeremiah's response about his ability and age say? (Jeremiah 1:6 Jeremiah didn't have any confidence in himself, so any work that was done would be clear evidence that the Lord was the one at work.)

4. What was God's perspective on Jeremiah's abilities or fears? (Jeremiah 1:7 God wasn't concerned about Jeremiah's abilities; only His willingness. The Lord promised His presence, His protection and His message. It only took one encounter with the Lord to make the task possible.)

5. What difference does the Lord's statement, "I have put my words in your mouth" make? (Jeremiah 1:9 Without the Lord's Word, Jeremiah has nothing to say and no authority with which to speak. It is God's Word alone that has authority over nations or kingdoms. It is His Word that destroys, builds and plants.)

6. What does the word "appoint" mean? (Jeremiah 1:5, 10 To "appoint" means to choose and select, which is what God did as He gave Jeremiah the role of Israel's prophet.)

Jonah
7. What is significant about Jonah's call? (Jonah 1:1-3 The Word of the Lord also came to Jonah. It was a difficult call because Nineveh was a large city, the people were wicked and they were Israel's enemies. Even though Jonah tried to run away, the Lord pursued him. He sent a storm and a fish; which spit Jonah out on the dry land. Jonah obeyed the Lord the second time, but he never cared about the people.)

8. How did Jonah try to get away from the Lord and His call? (Jonah 1:3, 5, 12 He tried to run the opposite way, he tried to hide in the bottom of the ship, he tried to sleep and he told them to throw him overboard, but none of them worked.)

9. How does the Lord's grace and mercy shine in this story? (Jonah 1:2, 4, 17; 2:10; 3:1, 10; 4:6, 8 The Lord's grace and mercy are the theme of this story. It is in God's mercy that the 120,000 people of Nineveh repented. It is in God's grace that the Lord spoke to Jonah. His grace is also visible in the wind, the great fish, the second call, the vine, the worm and the scorching east wind. Each of these actions by God was an opportunity for Jonah to repent and change his heart.)

10. How does the response of the sailors and, the pagan city, Nineveh compare to Jonah's? (Jonah 1:15-16; 3:5-6 When the sailors saw the power of God over the sea they worshiped Him. When the city heard the warning, they believed God, repented, declared a fast and put on sackcloth. Jonah did none of the above. His heart was hard and he didn't care about the people.)

11. Why did the sailors and the people of Nineveh worship and repent? (Jonah 1:15-16; 3:5-6 They feared the Lord, listened to the Word from Jonah, and believed in God.)

12. What was God's reaction to seeing the repentance of the Ninevites? (Jonah 3:10 When God saw what they did and how they turned from their evil ways, He had compassion and did not bring destruction upon them.)

13. Is Jonah in danger because of his attitude? (Jonah 4:1, 4, 8-10 Jonah is in danger of the same judgment as the Ninevites because he is angry at the Lord's compassion.)

14. Why did the Lord provide the vine for Jonah? (Jonah 4:6 To point out Jonah's bad attitude toward the people. Jonah cared more about the vine than he did about the 120,000 people.)

15. How does Jonah describe God's character based on seeing His compassion for Nineveh? (Jonah 4:2 Jonah described God as gracious and compassionate, slow to anger and abounding in love, a God who relents from sending calamity.)

16. How does this story relate to Jesus? (In Matthew 12:39-41 Jesus said that as Jonah was three days and nights in the fish, the Son of Man would be three days and nights in the earth.)

Application Questions:
Jeremiah
1. What is a call from God and how do you recognize it?
   (Jeremiah 1:4; Jonah 1:1-2 The call of God is a request from
   Him to do His work. It must come from the Word of the Lord
   and not our own ideas. It is an emphasis on what the Lord is
   doing through a person rather than on the person.)

2. Do you sense the Lord's calling you in your life? (Romans
   10:13-15 or "But you are a chosen people, a royal priesthood,
   a holy nation, a people belonging to God, that you may declare
   the praises of him who called you out of darkness into his
   wonderful light." 1 Peter 2:9)

3. Why can we have peace regarding the Lord's calling for us?
   (Jeremiah 1:5, 8 We can have peace in knowing that the Lord
   already knows what will happen, promises to be with us, and
   will rescue us in whatever we encounter.)

4. What kind of people is God able to use? How should this
   encourage us? (Jeremiah 1:6-7 God is able to use all people,
   young or old, great or small, which is encouraging because
   when we look at our lives, we feel inadequate for the work
   that God has set in front of us. The work has to do with the
   Lord rather than us.)

5. What is our faith based on when we look at our weaknesses
   and our problems? (Jeremiah 1:6-7 We are basing our faith on
   ourselves rather than on God. Our faith must trust in the Lord
   because He can do anything.)

Jonah
6. Does the Lord call us to do easy things? (Jonah 1:1-2 No, the
   Lord at times calls us to do things that seem impossible and
   undesirable.)

7. Can we ever run away from the Lord? Why or why not?
   (Jonah 1:3 No, we cannot run away from the Lord, but we can
   resist or rebel against His call for our lives.)

8. How is God's character essential for His calling? (Jonah 3:1
   (We need His grace and compassion. We need His second
   chances because we are sinful. Even when we fail and go our
   own way, the Lord is patient with us and pursues us. Apart

from His character we would be condemned like the Ninevites.)

9. When has the Lord given you a second chance?

10. How is the Lord able to use His Word when we are faithful preachers of it? (Jonah 3:4-5 The Lord is able to use His Word to transform lives. Sometimes the most unlikely people will repentance and believe.)

11. How have you seen the compassion of the Lord in your life?

12. How has God shown His compassion to all mankind through Jesus Christ? (Romans 5:8 "God demonstrates his own love for us in this: While we were still sinners, Christ died for us.")

13. How can the Lord's gift of the vine encourage us when we are having the wrong attitude towards the ministry that God has called us? (Jonah 4:6 In providing a vine for Jonah, we see God providing the shade and rest that Jonah needs. God demonstrates His compassion and faithfulness even when the task is hard. Thus, we can go forward in the ministry in confidence, knowing that the Lord will be with us.)

29. The Shepherd
1 Peter 5:1-10

1 Peter 5

1 To the elders among you, I appeal as a fellow elder, a witness of Christ's sufferings and one who also will share in the glory to be revealed:

2 Be shepherds of God's flock that is under your care, serving as overseers-- not because you must, but because you are willing, as God wants you to be; not greedy for money, but eager to serve;

3 not lording it over those entrusted to you, but being examples to the flock.

4 And when the Chief Shepherd appears, you will receive the crown of glory that will never fade away.

5 Young men, in the same way be submissive to those who are older. All of you, clothe yourselves with humility toward one another, because, "God opposes the proud but gives grace to the humble."

6 Humble yourselves, therefore, under God's mighty hand, that he may lift you up in due time.

7 Cast all your anxiety on him because he cares for you.

8 Be self-controlled and alert. Your enemy the devil prowls around like a roaring lion looking for someone to devour.

9 Resist him, standing firm in the faith, because you know that your brothers throughout the world are undergoing the same kind of sufferings.

10 And the God of all grace, who called you to his eternal glory in Christ, after you have suffered a little while, will himself restore you and make you strong, firm and steadfast.

Study Questions: The Shepherd
1 Peter 5:1-10

Introduction:
Jesus' view of leadership is different than how others often see it. Jesus used the illustration of a shepherd and said "I am the good shepherd. The good shepherd lays down his life for the sheep." (John 10:11) Peter used the same illustration as he talked to his fellow overseers. It is difficult for a pastor to serve the sheep that are under his care. They have problems and they have a mind of their own. At the same time there is no greater calling than to be serving God's flock.

Grace Goals:
Knowledge
- To understand the shepherding role of the pastor.
- To know that Jesus the Great Shepherd will be your reward.

Attitude
- To have a willing and eager attitude toward the ministry that the Lord has called you to.
- To be realistic about the challenges that the pastor faces.

Actions
- To humbly serve the Lord for His glory.
- To be wise and watchful shepherds, trusting God for strength.

Questions about the Text:
1. How does Peter start his appeal to the elders? (1 Peter 5:1
    a. He points out he, like them, is a fellow elder. He speaks as one brother to another rather than speaking with the authority of an apostle.
    b. He was a witness of Christ's sufferings, so he knows the risk of this calling and he knows the trials of leadership. His message carries the weight of the crucifixion.
    c. He also knows the resurrection and the promises Jesus gave to His disciples about the place He is preparing. He knows that the glory will be far greater than the suffering.)

2. What is the role of a shepherd of God's flock? (1 Peter 5:2
    a. It is a dirty calling. You care for people with messy lives. Many times the task is tiring and thankless. The

167

shepherd needs to care for, feed, carry, and lead His sheep.

b. It is a holy calling. This is the flock of God! He has called you to be His servant. He works through you and His flock looks up to you. You are the image of God that they identify with.)

3. How does Peter contrast the attitudes that people have toward the position ministry being a holy calling? (1 Peter 5:2-3
   a. There is a difference between the person fulfilling a duty and a person who is eager to serve. One is defined by the statement "I have to", the other is defined by the statement "I get to".
   b. There is a difference between someone who is greedy and someone who is giving. The greedy person thinks of themselves first; the giving person thinks of others first. Instead of loving things, they love God and ask others, "How can I help you?"
   c. There is a difference between a person who puts themselves over others and the one that sets the example for others. There is only one Lord, the rest of us are His servants. We are the one's called to wash people's feet and lifting them up.)

4. How is the appearing of the Chief Shepherd helpful? (1 Peter 5:4 The Chief Shepherd is the one that we serve. He is the reason that we have a calling and the reason we fulfill that calling. He is the one that rewards us with His crown of eternal glory, our reward is in heaven.)

5. Why does Peter emphasize humility? (1 Peter 5:5-6 Pride makes it impossible to lead God's flock. It is in humility that we reflect the attitude of Jesus who "did not consider equality with God something to be grasped, but made Himself nothing." The Lord will lift up the humble person and put down the proud person. Pride puts us in direct conflict with God because He alone is God.)

6. Peter gives practical instructions to his fellow elders. How are each helpful? (1 Peter 5:7-9
   a. First, give all your worries to the Lord. Worries, drain a person's energy and do not fix any problems. It is God's mighty hand that can fix problems and He is the one who cares for us.

     b. Second, watch out for the devil. He is looking for those who are weak, distracted, and vulnerable to destroy. Lions roar to scare their prey and cause them to run.

     c. Third, resist the devil by standing firm in the faith. Jesus defeated Satan on the cross, so he has no power except to frighten and accuse people. Standing firm in the faith of what Jesus has done is how Christians "brothers throughout the world" must stand.)

7. How can verse 10 encourage you? (1 Peter 5:10
     a. God has grace for you, more than you can measure. He will give you what you need.
     b. He has called you. He knows you, created you, and has this responsibility for you.
     c. Heaven is waiting for you. For now there will be problems, but there is a great goal ahead.
     d. He will restore you. It is His strength that makes ministry possible. He is the one that makes His servants strong, firm, and steadfast.)

Application Questions:
1. How does Peter's appeal relate to us? (1 Peter 5:1 As servants of God, we are all fellow workers for His kingdom. We did not witness Christ's sufferings first hand, but He suffered for our sin as well. We too must live in the hope of the resurrection and the promises of Jesus.)

2. What is our role as a shepherd of God's flock? (1 Peter 5:2
     a. The challenge of working with people is the same. It is messy, difficult, tiring and thankless. We too need to care for, feed, carry, and lead His sheep.
     b. The privilege of serving the Lord is the same. The Lord has called us to be His servants and in that we have a holy calling.)

3. When do these attitudes affect us? (1 Peter 5:2-3
     a. We can work for the Lord because it is our obligation. We might not say, "Do I have to?", but that attitude is just behind our actual words. When we serve him out of joy, it is exciting, an adventure.
     b. Greed can steal the joy of giving. The greedy person is actually losing more than they are gaining because

they think of themselves and miss the relationship with the other.

    c.   When we lift ourselves up we will ultimately fall. When we lift others up, we can watch them succeed.)

4.   What do you look forward to hear from the Chief Shepherd? (1 Peter 5:4 Well done, good and faithful servant?)

5.   Where do you struggle with pride? When has the Lord humbled you? (1 Peter 5:5-6 Paul said, I will boast all the more gladly about my weaknesses that Christ's power might rest on me.)

6.   How do you handle your worries? (1 Peter 5:7 Cast all your anxieties on Him because He cares for us.)

7.   Where are you vulnerable to the devil when he roars to scare you? (1 Peter 5:8)

8.   How could you resist the devil? (1 Peter 5:9 We are called to stand firm in the faith. It is also encouraging to hear, listen and read about the testimonies of other believers around the world.)

9.   How could you encourage someone with God's grace? (1 Peter 5:10)

10.   How did God's calling for ministry come to you?

11.   What do you look forward to in heaven?

12.   Where do you need the Lord's strength to do ministry?

30. The Servant
John 13:1-17

John 13

[1]It was just before the Passover Feast. Jesus knew that the time had come for him to leave this world and go to the Father. Having loved his own who were in the world, he now showed them the full extent of his love.

[2]The evening meal was being served, and the devil had already prompted Judas Iscariot, son of Simon, to betray Jesus. [3]Jesus knew that the Father had put all things under his power, and that he had come from God and was returning to God; [4]so he got up from the meal, took off his outer clothing, and wrapped a towel around his waist. [5]After that, he poured water into a basin and began to wash his disciples' feet, drying them with the towel that was wrapped around him.

[6]He came to Simon Peter, who said to him, "Lord, are you going to wash my feet?" [7]Jesus replied, "You do not realize now what I am doing, but later you will understand." [8] "No," said Peter, "you shall never wash my feet." Jesus answered, "Unless I wash you, you have no part with me." [9] "Then, Lord," Simon Peter replied, "not just my feet but my hands and my head as well!"

[10]Jesus answered, "A person who has had a bath needs only to wash his feet; his whole body is clean. And you are clean, though not every one of you." [11]For he knew who was going to betray him, and that was why he said not every one was clean.

[12]When he had finished washing their feet, he put on his clothes and returned to his place. "Do you understand what I have done for you?" he asked them. [13] "You call me 'Teacher' and 'Lord,' and rightly so, for that is what I am. [14]Now that I, your Lord and Teacher, have washed your feet, you also should wash one another's feet. [15]I have set you an example that you should do as I have done for you. [16]I tell you the truth, no servant is greater than his master, nor is a messenger greater than the one who sent him. [17]Now that you know these things, you will be blessed if you do them.

Study Questions: Being a Servant
John 13:1-17

Introduction:
A servant spirit is one of the hardest things for us to adopt in our lives. Our sinful flesh is filled with pride and self-centeredness. We often want to see ourselves recognized rather than to serve. However, God has a different calling for us. He says that if anyone is to be great he must become the servant of all. We are called to love our neighbor as ourselves. By doing so, we model Christ to them. In Philippians it says that Jesus took on the very nature of a servant. He served us by becoming obedient unto death and taking away our sins. Now we can serve others by giving them the forgiveness, hope, and grace of God.

Grace Goals:
Knowledge
- To understand that "whatever you did for one of the least of these brothers and sisters of mine, you did for me."
- To recognize the real needs that people have and pray that the Lord will give us His love for them.

Attitude
- To consider others as better than ourselves and to look to their interests before our own.
- To love our neighbors as ourselves.

Actions
- To serve others because Jesus served us first.
- To show practical tangible expressions of love.

Memory Verse:
Philippians 2:3-4 "Do nothing out of selfish ambition or vain conceit, but in humility consider others better than yourselves. Each of you should look not only to your own interests, but also to the interests of others."

Questions about the Story:
1. What was Jesus' purpose in washing the disciples feet? (John 13:1 Jesus wanted to show His disciples the full extent of His love.)

2. What is the full extent of His love? (John 13:1 The text refers to Jesus washing the disciples feet, but it is more than just water and a towel. Judas the betrayer and Peter the denier

172

were both among those whose feet Jesus had washed. The dirt of their feet was only surface deep. The dirt of each one's sins went to their heart.)

3. What is significant about the fact that they were celebrating Passover and that this event happened the night before Jesus was crucified? (John 13:1 Passover was the celebration of the time when the Angel of Death passed over the houses of the Israelites because they had sacrificed a lamb and put its blood on the door posts. Jesus was now becoming the final Passover lamb and His blood on the posts of our lives is what saves us from death. That is the full extent of His love.)

4. What did Jesus tell the disciples about God the Father? (John 13:3 Jesus told them that the Father had put all things under His power, He told them He had come from God and was returning to God.)

5. Even though Jesus had the power of the Father placed under Him, what did He decide to do for His disciples to show the full extent of His love for them? (John 13:4-5 Jesus took the role of a servant for His disciples as He took up a towel and a basin in order to wash and dry their feet.)

6. Why did Peter respond strongly to Jesus washing his feet? (John 13:6 Because Peter should have been washing Jesus' feet.)

7. Why does Jesus say Peter would have no part with Him? (John 13:8 Peter must learn and live the role of a servant. It is the way of the servant that makes us one with Jesus.)

8. Why did Jesus wash Judas' feet when He knew what Judas would do? (John 13:10-11 Jesus showed the full extent of His love by washing the feet of those who would betray Him. Jesus' love is unconditional. Jesus showed that to Judas, not wanting him to walk away, but to receive His grace.)

9. Why did Jesus set this example for the disciples? (John 13:13 So they could see that things are opposite in the kingdom of God. The "Teacher" or "Lord" is not above someone else, but rather they are the servant.)

10. What did Jesus command His disciples to do after He had washed their feet? (John 13:14 He told them that they should also wash one another's feet.)

11. What had Jesus given to His disciples? (John 13:15 Jesus had given them an example that they should do as He had done.)

12. What did Jesus tell His disciples regarding their obedience to His command? (John 13:17 You will be blessed if you serve.)

Application Questions:
1. How can we wash people's feet? (John 13:1 We can literally wash their feet, but more practically we can help them with anything that they need in their lives.)

2. How can we show people the full extent of Jesus love? (John 13:1 There are many ways that we can serve people, but the full extent of Jesus' love goes beyond helping people with their needs. His love means loving our enemies, giving sacrificially of ourselves and living Jesus to them.)

3. What does it mean for us that Jesus was the Passover lamb? (John 13:1 If Jesus is our Passover lamb it means that we do not have to fear death because the blood of Jesus protects us. It means that we are forgiven once and for all.)

4. If we are in some position of authority over someone else, what does this text have to say to us? (John 13:3-5, 13-14 If Jesus is our servant; then we are to be a servant of everyone. Mark 10:45)

5. How does it feel to be served? Would you respond like Peter? (John 13:6-9 It can feel uncomfortable or awkward to be served, especially if it is someone that we view as above us. It is also possible to let pride creep in and start to expect to be served or to take others for granted.)

6. Who is the role of serving to be for? (Everyone. Whether you have a high or low position, Jesus calls for all who are His disciples to take the role of servant. "For whoever exalts himself will be humbled, and whoever humbles himself will be exalted," Matthew 23:12.)

7. Is there any qualification as to who we are supposed to serve? How did Jesus treat the people around Him? (John 13:6-11 We are to be serving all men, even those who would try to refuse our service or those who hate us. Jesus calls us to love our enemies, to pray for them and to even to do good for them. In our prayers for them we are called to pray for their salvation and continually displaying Christ to them.)

8. Who are we a living example for?

9. What is your attitude toward serving? (Matthew 23:1-12; Luke 22:26-27; Philippians 2:3-11; Colossians 3:23-24; and 1 Peter 5:2)

10. What character is shown from your life when you are willing to be a servant to those around you?

11. What does the Lord promise will result from serving? (John 13:17 Jesus promises that we will be blessed if we serve. This blessing is ultimately the blessing of being Christ-like and serving your heavenly Father. See Matthew 18:1-4)

12. How can we serve those who God has placed around us?

31. The Sword
2 Timothy 3:16-4:5

2 Timothy 3

14 But as for you, continue in what you have learned and have become convinced of, because you know those from whom you learned it,

15 and how from infancy you have known the holy Scriptures, which are able to make you wise for salvation through faith in Christ Jesus.

16 All Scripture is God-breathed and is useful for teaching, rebuking, correcting and training in righteousness,

17 so that the man of God may be thoroughly equipped for every good work.

4:1 In the presence of God and of Christ Jesus, who will judge the living and the dead, and in view of his appearing and his kingdom, I give you this charge:

2 Preach the Word; be prepared in season and out of season; correct, rebuke and encourage-- with great patience and careful instruction.

3 For the time will come when men will not put up with sound doctrine. Instead, to suit their own desires, they will gather around them a great number of teachers to say what their itching ears want to hear.

4 They will turn their ears away from the truth and turn aside to myths.

5 But you, keep your head in all situations, endure hardship, do the work of an evangelist, discharge all the duties of your ministry.

Study Questions: The Sword
2 Timothy 3:16-4:5

Introduction:
The Word of God is the sword of the Spirit. It is the primary tool of the pastor for His people. It is the authority and the power of God. The Word is what the people desperately need to hear. It is living and active. The Word brings the spiritually dead to life in Christ. It is the living water for the weary and it is the sword that cuts into the joints and marrow of the proud. Oh praise Almighty God for giving us His Word.

Grace Goals:
Knowledge
– To know the value of the Word of God.
– To understand how the Law cuts and the Gospel heals.

Attitude
– To trust God's Word and have full confidence in it.
– To care about our people enough to feed them well.

Actions
– To be prepared to use the Word in season and out of season.
– To personally take time daily for the Word of God.

Questions about the Text:
1. What is Paul's encouragement to young pastor Timothy? (2 Timothy 3:14-15 He tells him to continue in Scripture. He learned it and has become convinced of it. His teachers were trustworthy. His mother and grandmother brought him up in the Word and he grew in faith in Jesus that lead him to salvation.)

2. What is the difference between physical battles and spiritual battles? (2 Timothy 3:14-17 Spiritual battles have to do with the unseen things of the mind, heart, and spirit. They have to do with eternity, sin, grace, and mercy.)

3. What does it mean that "all Scripture is God-breathed?" (2 Timothy 3:16 It means that all of the Scriptures are the very words of God. It is His breath that brings life. It is His desire to reveal Himself and to communicate with us.)

4. How does Scripture enable a person to fight spiritual battles?
    (2 Timothy 3:14-16 Scripture is God breathed. It is powerful
    in itself. It is able to teach us about God and man. It is able to
    make us wise and grow in faith. It can teach, rebuke, correct,
    and train. These are all a part of the unseen areas of life where
    the spiritual battles rage.)

5. What are some examples of how Scripture teaches, rebukes,
    corrects, and trains in righteousness? (2 Timothy 3:16
    a. Teach – It shows us who God is and what He expects
    b. Rebuke – It reveals our sin and warns us of judgment
    c. Correct – It brings us back to Jesus
    d. Train in Righteousness – It develops us in an outward
        and inward reflection of Jesus.)

6. Why does Paul give such a solemn charge? (2 Timothy 4:1
    The responsibility of a pastor is to work with spiritual matters,
    life and death, heaven and hell. This responsibility is great and
    should not be taken lightly. If we stand on our own we are
    desperately vulnerable, but we can stand on God's solid Word.
    When it is God's Word that we use to point out sin then it is
    no longer us judging but it is the Word of God.)

7. How is the pastor's primary task to be lived out? (2 Timothy
    4:2 They are to preach the Word at all times and in all ways.
    That task requires being prepared in every season. The two
    aspects of the preaching are the Law and the gospel. People
    need the correction and rebuke of the law. They also need the
    encouragement, the patient grace, and the careful instruction
    of the gospel.)

8. Why is the Word such an important tool for the pastor?
    (2 Timothy 4:3-4 Because man's heart wants to feed itself on
    all of its own desires. The heart of man will find people who
    will say whatever it wants to hear. God's Word has the
    authority and power to convict, correct, and convert the heart
    of man.)

9. In contrast to the deceitful heart of man, how can the Word be
    helpful for the pastor himself? (2 Timothy 4:5 The Word is a
    sure foundation on which to base his thoughts. It gives him the
    strength and the motivation to endure hardships. It is the tool

of the evangelist to bring salvation, and it is source for all of the duties of ministry.)

Application Questions:
1. How did you learn about scriptures and who were those who influenced you along the way?

2. What scriptures influenced you to come to faith in the Lord?

3. What spiritual battles do you face? (2 Timothy 3:14-17 Spiritual battles can include doubts, fears, failures, acceptance and temptations. They include anything that controls you apart from Christ.)

4. What Scriptures breath the life of God into you? (2 Timothy 3:16 Any Scripture that God uses to fill you with the revelation of Himself, the joy of His salvation, and His presence with you can be a part of the life that in turn breath into other people's lives as well.)

5. Which Scriptures help you fight spiritual battles that you face? (2 Timothy 3:14-16 Scriptures that show us our sin, cause us to turn to Jesus, and know how to live are all useful to face the battles in our own life as well as the word that we would share with others.)

6. What are some examples of Scriptures that people around you need to hear? (2 Timothy 3:16
   a. Teach –
   b. Rebuke –
   c. Correct –
   d. Train in Righteousness –)

7. When have you felt the solemn responsibility of sharing God's Word accurately? (2 Timothy 4:1)

8. What does good sermon preparation look like for you? (2 Timothy 4:2 Knowing the Word personally. Learning the scripture for Sunday far in advance. Knowing the needs of the people. Connecting the knowledge of the Word with the application for the people.)

9. When can you use the Word as you speak into people's lives? (2 Timothy 4:3-4 When people think that they are "good

enough" or "better than others" they need the Law to convict them of sin. When people feel hopeless, helpless, or worthless they need the Gospel promises of God.)

10. When do you allow the Word of God to speak into your own life? (2 Timothy 4:5 The pastor must have a personal devotion time where they meet with God daily.)

32. The Family
John 19:25-27 & Luke 15:11-32

John 19
25Near the cross of Jesus stood his mother, his mother's sister, Mary the wife of Clopas, and Mary Magdalene. 26When Jesus saw his mother there, and the disciple whom he loved standing nearby, he said to his mother, "Dear woman, here is your son," 27and to the disciple, "Here is your mother." From that time on, this disciple took her into his home.

Luke 15
11Jesus continued: "There was a man who had two sons. 12The younger one said to his father, 'Father, give me my share of the estate.' So he divided his property between them.

13"Not long after that, the younger son got together all he had, set off for a distant country and there squandered his wealth in wild living. 14After he had spent everything, there was a severe famine in that whole country, and he began to be in need. 15So he went and hired himself out to a citizen of that country, who sent him to his fields to feed pigs. 16He longed to fill his stomach with the pods that the pigs were eating, but no one gave him anything.

17"When he came to his senses, he said, 'How many of my father's hired men have food to spare, and here I am starving to death! 18I will set out and go back to my father and say to him: Father, I have sinned against heaven and against you. 19I am no longer worthy to be called your son; make me like one of your hired men.' 20So he got up and went to his father.

"But while he was still a long way off, his father saw him and was filled with compassion for him; he ran to his son, threw his arms around him and kissed him.

21"The son said to him, 'Father, I have sinned against heaven and against you. I am no longer worthy to be called your son.'

22"But the father said to his servants, 'Quick! Bring the best robe and put it on him. Put a ring on his finger and sandals on his feet. 23Bring the fattened calf and kill it. Let's have a feast and celebrate. 24For this son of mine was dead and is alive again; he was lost and is found.' So they began to celebrate.

181

²⁵"Meanwhile, the older son was in the field. When he came near the house, he heard music and dancing. ²⁶So he called one of the servants and asked him what was going on. ²⁷'Your brother has come,' he replied, 'and your father has killed the fattened calf because he has him back safe and sound.'

²⁸"The older brother became angry and refused to go in. So his father went out and pleaded with him. ²⁹But he answered his father, 'Look! All these years I've been slaving for you and never disobeyed your orders. Yet you never gave me even a young goat so I could celebrate with my friends. ³⁰But when this son of yours who has squandered your property with prostitutes comes home, you kill the fattened calf for him!'

³¹" 'My son,' the father said, 'you are always with me, and everything I have is yours. ³²But we had to celebrate and be glad, because this brother of yours was dead and is alive again; he was lost and is found.'"

Introduction:
As Jesus hung dying on the cross, His concern was the care for His mother more than Himself. As Jesus spoke to John and Mary, He was caring for her earthly needs by entrusting her to John's care and He was caring for her eternal needs by dying on the cross. That type of love is unconditional, it does not matter what the other person has done. It is giving love that is not concerned with what is received in return. Unconditional love is also described in the text from Luke 15 of the two lost sons. Both of the two boys had conditional love. They were selfish and self-centered and it was the father that had to go to them and bring them back into the family.

God has also given each of us a family to care for. We carry responsibilities for our parents, spouses and children. The first responsibility is to love them as Christ loved the Church; which was even unto death. His ultimate unconditional love is what makes it possible to for us to selflessly love our own families.

Grace Goals:
Knowledge
- To understand the unconditional love that God has for us that we would be called His children.
- To recognize that God is our Heavenly Father and we, in Christ, are a part of His family.
- To remember our God-given responsibilities to our families and their need to be loved.

Attitude
- To praise the Lord for the immediate family members that He has given us.
- To love all of our brothers and sisters in the Lord who make up the body of Christ, "the family of God."

Actions
- To serve, provide for, respect, and love those who are a part of our immediate family.
- To forgive, offer grace and sacrifice for them as well.

Memory Verse:
Mark 3:35 "Whoever does God's will is my brother and sister and mother."

Questions about the Text:

1. What do those at the cross say with just their presence? (John 19:25-26 They loved Jesus, they believed in Him and they were grieving together.)

2. Why did Jesus direct His mother to John and John to His mother? (John 19:26-27 Jesus gave John the responsibility of her care; which would have been the first born son's role. Jesus also entrusted John into His mother's care because he also needed her.)

3. What does John's response show? (John 19:27 John was faithful to his responsibility and Mary also cared for John.)

4. What does it mean when the younger son asks the father for his estate? (Luke 15:12-13 The younger son is saying that he ultimately cares more about money than the family. By asking for the inheritance, which is given at a person's death, he also says that he wanted the inheritance of his father's death.)

5. By giving the son the inheritance, what does the father communicate? (Luke15:12 He loved the son, but could not force his son to love him in return.)

6. What did the son learn after squandering his wealth? (Luke 15:13-16 He learned that riches don't last, that he needed help and that he needed his family. He also learned that you cannot buy love or happiness.)

7. What did his hunger, disgrace and emptiness show him? (Luke 15:14-19 It showed him that he had it great back home, that he had sinned, that he needed his father's forgiveness and that he didn't deserve anything.)

8. How were the problems that he had faced a blessing to him? (Luke 15:17-19 The son came to his senses with a repentant heart. He saw that he was unworthy of anything.)

9. What does the son's speech say? (Luke 15:18-19 His sin was against God and it showed his heart. He expected to be treated like a hired hand or a servant.)

10. What is unusual about the father's response? Why? (Luke 15:20-24 The father had been watching for him. He was filled

with compassion, ran to the son, called his servants to bring a robe, a ring, and sandals, to kill the fatted calf, and to call a celebration feast. The son was "dead" and was alive again, he was lost and had been found. The father showed undeserved extravagant love and mercy for the younger son.)

11. What does the older son's response say? Why? (Luke 15:25 The older son was angry and bitter. He was holding a grudge against his brother. He was also proud and self-centered.)

12. Why did the father go out to meet the older son and ask him to come in? (Luke 15:28-32 The Father loved him as well. The father desired the family to be together, not separated.)

Application Questions:
1. How can we support our family in their trials? (John 19:25 Going through trials with them often says more than words.)

2. What responsibilities do we have for our families? (John 19:26-27 Care for our parents, spouse and children is a high priority. As we love them, we love the Lord.)

3. Is your love for your family like Christ's love for the church? (Jesus' love for the church is both sacrificial and unconditional. That type of love lived out in the family establishes boundaries that must be obeyed but they are enforced within an unconditional relationship. Ephesians 5:22, 25, 6:1)

4. Should we only love our family when we are in a situation that makes it easy to love them? (No, we see that Jesus showed love for His family when He was hanging on the cross and ready to die. The father welcomed the prodigal son home even after the son had left him and wasted his money. "For if you forgive men when they sin against you, your heavenly Father will also forgive you." Matthew 6:14)

5. How do we waste the riches that our Father in heaven has given to us? (Luke 15:12-13 We, like the older son, try to hoard God's resources for ourselves. We care more about ourselves than we do about God or His family. We try to buy happiness and love and we waste His gifts.)

185

6. What trials does the Lord allow into our lives to show us our need of Him? (Luke 15:14-16 He allows pain to come in many forms when we run away from Him. Emotional and physical pain can serve as reminders to cause us to come to our senses.)

7. What is your memory of your father?

8. How is the Lord like the prodigal's father? (Luke 15:20 The Heavenly Father is looking for and longing for His children to come to Him. He is filled with compassion and undeserved love.)

9. What prepared speeches have we tried to give to the Lord like the prodigal son did to his father?

10. When does the Lord see us in our need? (Luke 15:20 Even while we are far off.)

11. What is the Father's response to us when we come to Him in need? (Luke 15:32 He runs out to meet us, wraps His arms around us and welcomes us into His family.)

12. When we see God's undeserved grace on someone else's life, what is our response? (Luke 15:27-28)

13. How are we often like the older son? (Luke 15:28-30 We can complain or hold grudges because things are not fair.)

14. How is your relationship with your parents, spouse or children? (Ephesians 5:22-33; 6:4)

15. How can you show sacrificial and unconditional love to your spouse and your children? (Talk, work, pray and eat together. Put their needs before your own.)

16. How do you provide for your family? (1 Timothy 5:8)

17. What would your Heavenly Father say to you right now?

33. The Neighbors
Luke 10:25-37

Luke 10

²⁵On one occasion an expert in the law stood up to test Jesus. "Teacher," he asked, "what must I do to inherit eternal life?"

²⁶"What is written in the Law?" he replied. "How do you read it?"

²⁷He answered: " 'Love the Lord your God with all your heart and with all your soul and with all your strength and with all your mind'; and, 'Love your neighbor as yourself.'"

²⁸"You have answered correctly," Jesus replied. "Do this and you will live."

²⁹But he wanted to justify himself, so he asked Jesus, "And who is my neighbor?"

³⁰In reply Jesus said: "A man was going down from Jerusalem to Jericho, when he fell into the hands of robbers. They stripped him of his clothes, beat him and went away, leaving him half dead. ³¹A priest happened to be going down the same road, and when he saw the man, he passed by on the other side. ³²So too, a Levite, when he came to the place and saw him, passed by on the other side. ³³But a Samaritan, as he traveled, came where the man was; and when he saw him, he took pity on him. ³⁴He went to him and bandaged his wounds, pouring on oil and wine. Then he put the man on his own donkey, took him to an inn and took care of him. ³⁵The next day he took out two silver coins and gave them to the innkeeper. 'Look after him,' he said, 'and when I return, I will reimburse you for any extra expense you may have.'

³⁶"Which of these three do you think was a neighbor to the man who fell into the hands of robbers?"

³⁷The expert in the law replied, "The one who had mercy on him."
Jesus told him, "Go and do likewise."

Study Questions: The Neighbors
Luke 10:25-37

Introduction:

The expert in the Law could mentally understand and even agree with the need to love God and to love others, but the extent to which Jesus described love was beyond what seemed reasonable. To love a dying stranger or to use a Samaritan as the example of love went too far.

Loving some neighbors may be easy because of the friendship we have or the benefits we receive. The love that Jesus suggests is caring for people we don't know, those who could never pay us back and even for our enemies. It is in this extravagant love that Jesus is revealed. This is the type of love that He demonstrated to us. Jesus is the one that carried us, healed us and paid a debt that we could not repay. To love our neighbors is just showing them what we have first received. In Matthew 25:40, Jesus said, "Whatever you did for one of the least of these brothers of Mine, you did for Me."

Grace Goals:

Knowledge
- To understand that our love for others comes from the wellspring of love that the Lord has lavished on us.
- To realize that showing love is a daily choice and opportunity.

Attitude
- To have Jesus' love for people, no matter their age, race, appearance, or background.
- To consider others better than ourselves.

Actions
- To look for those who need Christ's love and compassion.
- To give others the selfless sacrificial love that Christ gave us.

Memory Verse:

1 John 4:7-9 "Dear friends, let us love one another, for love comes from God. Everyone who loves has been born of God and knows God. Whoever does not love does not know God, because God is love. This is how God showed His love among us: He sent His one and only Son into the world that we might live through Him."

Questions about the Text:

1. How did the expert of the Law's test backfire on him? (Luke 10:25, 37 He wanted to justify himself or prove that he was right. Instead, Jesus' story pointed out how wrong he was.)

2. What does the question, "What must I do to inherit eternal life?" assume? (Luke 10:25 It assumes that if we do enough or if we do the right things, then we will inherit eternal life.)

3. Why did the man ask the question about how to inherit eternal life if he knew the answer? (Luke 10:26-27 He knew that it was difficult to follow the Law perfectly. Jesus made sure that he knew that it was impossible to keep the law.)

4. How could the man show his love for an unseen God? (Luke 10:27 He could show a sincere love for God by loving those created in God's image.)

5. What is the difference between the robbers, the priest and the Levite? (Luke 10:30-32 The robbers were physically violent toward the man from their evil nature. The priest and Levite uncaring and unconcerned toward the man which also came from their evil nature.)

6. Why did the priest and Levite pass by on the other side of the man? (Luke 10:31-32 They were religious men with high prominence in society. To come across a dead man meant that they would be unclean. They cared more about their religious cleanliness more than the person made in God's image.)

7. How did the Samaritan show love when he saw the injured man? (Luke 10:33-34 He took pity on him, treated and bandaged his wounds. The Samaritan also put the man on his own donkey, took him to an inn, and took care of him.)

8. Why did the Samaritan give the innkeeper payment and promise to give him more? (Luke 10:35 The Samaritan was more concerned about the man than about himself.)

9. What does the Samaritan's response reveal? (Luke 10:33-35 It showed the genuine love that the man had in his heart. It revealed that the priest and the Levite were not showing love.

He demonstrated the extent to which God has loved us.)

10. Why did Jesus ask the expert in The Law "who do you think was a neighbor?" (Luke 10:37 It revealed his lack of love for people and his hard heart toward God. The man couldn't even say the word Samaritan because of his hard heart.)

Application Questions:

1. Similar to the expert of the law, how do we desire to "do things" in order to inherit eternal life in our lives?

2. Where do we need to find our love? (Luke 10:26 Our love comes from Jesus. He loved us extravagantly. He is the one that carried us, healed us and paid a debt that we could not repay. To love our neighbors is showing them what we have first received. 1 John 4:19 says, "We love them because He first loved us.")

3. How can we practically love God and love people? (Luke 10:27 When we stop and see people's needs, meet those needs, share their burden and give of ourselves.)

4. Why are we to "love our neighbor" and why is it difficult? (Luke 10:27, 37 We are to love them because the Lord commanded us and because God is love. It is difficult because it is against our nature to love others. It is only Jesus love in us that is anything besides selfish.)

5. What are some ways that we act like the robbers, the priest or the Levite? (Luke 10:30-32 We take advantage of people without being concerned about them. We walk by people without thinking about their needs, their hurts, or how we could help them. Our schedule or our reputation is more important than another's needs.)

6. How do we reflect the love of God when we show others love? (Luke 10:33-35 We reflect God's love when we care about people regardless of whom they are and regardless of any thought about ourselves.)

7. How does our "position" affect who we choose to help? (We can feel it would degrade us to stoop down and help someone.

We can think of ourselves more highly than we ought.)

8. What does it mean to love your neighbor? (Matthew 7:12 says, "In everything, do to others what you would have them do to you.")

9. What should be our response to this parable? (Luke 10:33 Asking the Lord's forgiveness for hurting and walking by people and asking Him to give us His love for the neighbors that I pass every day.)

10. Does Jesus share this story with the man to reveal a way for man to attain eternal life? (Yes and no, Jesus is showing the man and us that we will continually fall short of keeping the whole Law and that attaining eternal life has nothing to do with our works but a pleading of forgiveness of sins by the blood of Jesus.)

Appendix - History of the Ambassador Institute

The question that had been on my mind for a long time was, "How can you train people from multiple backgrounds and languages in the Word of God?" I had been confronted with that challenge in Tanzania while working with the evangelists who had been entrusted with leading their churches. The barriers for them to be trained in God's Word were many including: language, finances, family responsibilities, availability of training, training resources, and learning styles.

It was a little old lady from a small Wisconsin church that the Lord used to introduce me to the International Orality Network. It was revealing to consider that the training method that Jesus used to train His own disciples could still be used to train people in God's Word today. It is striking to consider that the parables and questions that Jesus used make it possible to jump language and culture now. The college trained and the illiterate are able to interact together when an oral style of training is used.

That began an experiment that has grown to become a reality with amazing results that are only explainable by the hand of God. The first group of 20 students started training in Uganda and after the first class had completed their two years of studies, they began seven more classes and those same students began teaching the second generation. The second graduation included 71 students and those students started 20 classes with the hope of seeing 300 in the next graduation.

This book is the result of something that the Lord has been doing over the past five years. It is the combined effort of people from six countries. Some have taught and applied the training, others have translated, others have check for doctrinal integrity and others for grammatical accuracy. Pastor Nate Jore, a missionary to Uganda, has led the way in putting this curriculum into practice. He has given his life and God's Word into the hands of Ugandan leaders and the Lord has used him to multiply this training. Nathan Olson and Andrew Olson have expanded this work so that it is available in Portuguese, Spanish and Luganda, Pastor Valery Hryhoryk has done the Russian translation and Pastor Devasahayam Dunna has been leading the Telugu translation and work in India.

All of this has been done for the purpose of training people in God's Word and it is for His Glory. No single person can take credit for what has happened and how the Lord has used this to expand His Kingdom. "What, after all, is Apollos? And What is Paul? Only servants, through whom you came to believe – as the Lord has assigned to each His task. By the grace God has given me, I laid a foundation… and someone else is building on it. But each one should be careful how he builds. For no one can lay any foundation other than the one already laid, which is Jesus Christ." 1 Corinthians 3:5, 10-11

Pastor Kevin Olson
Ambassador Institute Department Head

Proof

Made in the USA
Columbia, SC
29 May 2018